Counseling an

Counseling and Theology

William E. Hulme

FORTRESS PRESS PHILADELPHIA

First Fortress Paperback edition 1967

Library of Congress Catalog Card Number 56-5643

4026K66 Printed in U.S.A. 1-1780

Table of Contents

I. Counseling and Theology 1

II. The Need for a Listener 19

III. The Need for Confession 39

IV. The Need for Understanding 58

V. The Need for Growth 79

VI. The Concept of Man 95

VII. The Concept of the Universal Priesthood . . 115

VIII. The Concept of Freedom 131

IX. The Means of Acceptance 150

X. The Means of Growth 177

XI. The Means of Grace
1. The Scripture in Counseling 202

XII. The Means of Grace
2. The Sacrement in Counseling 226

CHAPTER ONE

Counseling and Theology

Pastoral counseling in its present form is a new development within the church. Pastors who have celebrated the twenty-fifth anniversary of their ordination heard little if anything about it in their seminary days. Pastoral counseling is also a popular movement within the church. We see this in the many books that have been published on the subject in recent years, by the appearance of periodicals such as *Pastoral Psychology* and *The Journal of Pastoral Care*, by the Pastoral Psychology Book Club, by the emergence of centers for clinical training for theological students and pastors such as the Council for Clinical Training and the Institute of Pastoral Care, by the addition of courses in counseling in theological seminaries, by the increasingly frequent appearance of pastoral counseling on the programs of pastoral conferences and seminars, and by the increase in emphasis on the counseling ministry within the local parish.

ORIENTED IN PSYCHOLOGY

Although pastoral counseling is new in its form it is not new in its purpose. The care and cure of souls is as old as the church. The German term *seelsorge* (soul care) for example, has a history that dates back to the Reformation and even before. In former days the pastor's counseling was oriented in pastoral theology; today it centers in pastoral psychology. The impetus for the new movement has come more from the laboratories of the psychological sciences than from the scholarship of theologians. It is a psychologically oriented *seelsorge.*

In a broad sense modern psychotherapy has its origin in the Freudian era of depth psychology and the psychoanalytic method. Freud's work was revolutionary in the world of science and he drew more than his share of criticism. The church joined in this criticism, not so much for Freud's science as for his philosophy. Freud was a mechanistic determinist who saw religion as an illusion—a projection of the father image—serving as a temporary crutch. A genuinely mature person would outgrow the need for religion. Despite his outstanding success in the treatment of neurotic people, Freud was a pessimist regarding human nature. In his interpretation of his data he formulated a doctrine of personality that outdid the doctrine of original sin.

The passing of time and the subsiding of emotions have made possible a more objective analysis of Freud's work. The consensus seems to be that his interpretation of the cause of personality disorders is too limited. Analysts Adler, Jung, Rank, Horney, Alexander and others have sought in their distinctive ways to expand the Freudian interpretation, and all have emphasized the social setting in addition to the inner dynamics of the orthodox Freudian school. The psychoanalytic method, however, in bringing to the surface the repressed memories and impulses of the past, has proved to be one of the most important milestones in the history of psychotherapy. Because of its intense thoroughness, however, the method has been modified in the laboratories of clinical psychology into more available modes of psychotherapy such as counseling. Counseling techniques have been developed with considerable experimentation by the laboratories of clinical psychology. Accompanying these psychological advances has been the increasing exploration on the part of the medical profession into psychosomatic illnesses and the psychiatric approach in psychosomatic medicine. These developments have aroused a general interest in psychotherapy in our times and in particular among the clergy.

INCORPORATED INTO THE OFFICE OF THE MINISTRY

Psychotherapy in all of its methods is dealing with the same basic problems of human nature as is the Christian religion. It is only natural that this parallel would not long go unnoticed. The church is indebted to the pioneers in its ranks who saw the value of the expanding data of psychotherapy for the pastor. One of these, Anton T. Boisen, gained his incentive from his own experience of and recovery from mental illness. It was his work that gave rise to the Council for Clinical Training. These pioneers and those they inspired to follow in their steps have succeeded in adapting the principles of psychotherapy into the framework of the ministry so well that we have today in pastoral counseling a field of study that is distinct from other areas of psychotherapy and is rapidly developing into a science in its own right.

Even in its present stage of rapid development, pastoral counseling is more unified as a science than is its foster parent, clinical psychology, which is openly divided into conflicting schools of thought. Leaders in pastoral counseling are reluctant to identify themselves with any particular method of counseling and refuse even to label their own approach. Nonetheless there is a trend among the majority of these leaders toward a client-centered counseling. Since he published his *Counseling and Psychotherapy* in 1942, Carl Rogers has taken the lead among clinical psychologists in client-centered therapy. His approach is based on the work of Rank, who broke with Freud and sought to free psychoanalysis from its complexity to make it available for a counseling relationship. His pupil, Jessie Taft, worked in a similar direction. Some of the leaders in pastoral counseling consider the client-centered therapy of Rogers extreme and have modified it to fit into their particular concept of the pastoral role, while others have taken it as it is and given it a religious setting. Of late there has been a shift in emphasis to the inner attitudes of the counselor and to the relationship or communication between the counselor and the counselee, but this has merely expanded rather than altered the principles of client-centered therapy.[1]

PASTORS AND CLIENT-CENTERED THERAPY

Rogers represents only one school of thought in the field of counseling. There are others who advocate a more directive approach, for example F. C. Thorne, the editor of the *Journal of Clinical Psychology*. Yet this directive approach receives scant attention from the leaders of pastoral counseling, perhaps because Rogers asks little of the counselor; he need not be a psychologist. The responsibility for the solution to the problem, as well as for the control of the interview, rests with the counselee. The method therefore fits in well with a professional group whose training is not usually in the field of psychology.

Perhaps a more significant possibility is that the pastor has heretofore been guilty of anything but a client-centered approach in his counseling. His present interest in pastoral counseling in part grows out of his awareness that the pastor is

[1] Cf. Carroll Wise, *Pastoral Counseling, Its Theory and Practice* (New York: Harper, 1951), for the emphasis on the relationship between the counselor and counselee; and Seward Hiltner, *The Counselor in Counseling* (Nashville: Abingdon, 1952), for a concentration on the inner dynamics of the personality of the counselor in the counseling process.

not the successful counselor that he should be. It is only natural that he should react against any method that is associated with this past failure. I remember attending a pastoral conference where the "Rogers Method" of counseling was on the program. During the discussion that followed the presentation it was evident that the group was unsympathetic toward the method and the speaker felt it necessary to retreat somewhat from his original stand. Things changed completely, however, when a certain pastor arose and said, "I am not a bit afraid that we will go off the deep end on nondirective counseling [as it was called at that time]—not with the seminary training *we* received. In fact I think a little of the Rogers Method would be a wholesome influence for all of us."

A third possibility is that pastoral counseling has its origin primarily among those of the liberal religious movement within Protestantism which has a natural resistance toward any authoritative attitude based on the traditions of the past. The client-centered approach breaks with set patterns of thought and practice. It compels the pastor to set aside, at least for the time being, his own value judgments as he acknowledges the sentiments of the counselee. There is no attempt to rid the pastor of his convictions but only to prevent these convictions from controlling the interview. As we shall see in later chapters this temporary setting aside of the pastor's opinions ultimately works out better for these opinions than were he to press them into the picture from the start. Yet because this paradox is hidden beneath the surface, many pastors are confused over the new movement and even view it with some degree of suspicion.

COUNSELING AND THE THEOLOGY OF THE CHURCH

These ministers are usually those of the more conservative element within the church. And they have something to conserve. When we look at the church in its present moment we are looking at it from its top side. We do not get the complete view of the church until we see it in terms of its historical development through the ages. A vital part of this development is the religious heritage that for want of a better name we shall call the theology of the church. Although this heritage comes from the past it is inseparable from the forms of worship, hymns, and articles of faith that are in use at the present time in the churches.

Pastoral counseling however with its psychological orientation has developed alongside of rather than within the framework of this theology. And no wonder! To many of the leaders of the new movement this religious heritage has been associated with a form of pastoral care that they now feel is bankrupt. Yet to the conservative pastor this gap between the two only increases his confusion. He knows that the theology of the church emerged as an answer to the problems which beset the pastoral counselor. It is likely that the majority of the pastors of America are of this more conservative bent and their difficulties over the new movement are preventing the full endorsement of its principles which the problems of their people demand. I believe the time has come in the rise of pastoral counseling when this conflict must be faced and some attempt made to solve it. Otherwise the growing interest in the new movement may reach a point where because of this conflict it can go no further. It is even possible that the movement itself may become an issue of dissension within the church rather than the means for unity which I am convinced it can be.

The trouble with the theology of the church is that it is old. Not that age in itself is discrediting. A liberalism that rejects the old simply because it is old is no longer liberal but prejudiced. As the theology of the church has become old, however, people have also become old to it. What is alive in one age may become merely an ornament in the next. We notice this particularly among churches that emphasize liturgy and creeds. In the wake of the experience that gave rise to the symbols of religion lies the danger of dead orthodoxy and form-for-form's-sake observance. Yet eliminating the forms does not eliminate the danger. Even the Society of Friends, so sensitive to the abuse of forms that they divorced their religion from these forms, faces the same lethargy. In his *Testament of Devotion* Thomas Kelley laments that many of his Quaker brethren have become as conventional as the people against whom their forefathers rebelled.[2] Whether forms are good or bad is not the question since the human mind is bound to formulize. Even the inner light and silent worship are forms and can become traditional and dead.

The need for articles of faith is the need for the verbalization of inner experience. As we shall see in later chapters this communication of inner experience is the basis of the counseling process. In addition these articles also are symbols of solidarity, giving expression to the like-mindedness of the group and to the security of belonging. The confession of the creed during a worship service deepens the experience of the communion of saints; its tie is not only horizontal but also vertical as it joins the believer with the church of history and the church in glory. There is always the danger however that these articles may neither engender nor express the human experience of former generations.

The close relationship between the principles of pastoral counseling and the dynamics of the human personality make it very unlikely that the new movement is something of a fad that will sooner or later run its course. In view of the evi-

[2] Thomas Kelley, *A Testament of Devotion* (New York: Harper, 1941), p. 53.

dence from history of the great pastors of the past it is equally unlikely that effective pastoral counseling came into existence in the post-Freudian era of the twentieth century. These successful ministers of former days used the theology of the church in their counseling. Although our present age is highly productive of the problems of personality, we are dealing with the same old human nature. The principles of counseling used by these pastors of the ages can scarcely be meaningless to the problems of today.

We can understand why many of the leaders of the new movement have not understood this meaning from the past. Those who seek to conserve sometimes only confine. The revelation that became incarnate in human experience has to many become divorced from this experience. The successors of the great churchmen of the past have too often communicated the doctrines of the church in a legalistic fashion that had little relation to the dynamics of the human personality. The result is an overintellectualized religion that is unable to reach the deep emotional conflicts of life. Such a religion plays into the hands of those who would rather rationalize than resolve these conflicts.

CURRENT THEOLOGICAL MOVEMENTS

This legalistic approach may also be a reason why confessional theology as it is formulated in the denominational articles of faith plays a relatively small role in the contemporary theological picture. Instead we have opposing theological movements of comparatively recent origin which not only cut across denominational lines but may also be found within a single denomination. It seems presumptuous to discuss these movements in a few words when books have been written on each of them. However our purpose is merely to see the effect of these movements upon the contemporary theological scene and consequently an exhaustive treatment is not necessary.

The first of these in point of origin is liberal theology. Normally we think of this movement as a reaction against confessional theology. Actually however it began more as a reaction against the legalistic presentation of confessional theology. The liberal feels that God works through human processes within the individual and through the laws of nature in the universe. God is immanent in his world and his ways are more comprehensible to human reason than former generations believed. The liberal believes in the inherent potential within the individual to improve himself and his society. He is gaining an increased respect however for the recalcitrance of human nature and for the complexity of the task of creating the kingdom of God on earth. The changes within its own history and the critical spirit which its proponents turn also upon their own positions show there is nothing static about liberal theology.

Fundamentalism emerged as a reaction against liberalism. The fundamentalist belligerently took up his cudgels for the adherence to right doctrine. He accuses the liberals of reducing God to the limitations of human reason and he in turn is accused by them of a rigid conception of religion. Since the liberals gained their ground within the universities and theological seminaries the fundamentalists in the early years of the controversy established their own Bible institutes for the education of their youth. Because of this their opponents considered their position below the intellectually respectable. However this situation is changing. Fundamentalism has its scholars even as do the other schools of interpretation.

The third movement had its beginnings in Kierkegaard and came into its own as a theology in the Europe following the first World War. Called Barthian after its leading exponent in Europe, and neo-orthodox because of its similarity to the old theology, the movement took hold also in America largely through the leadership of Reinhold Niebuhr. Neo-orthodoxy is also a reaction against liberalism, not in defense of historic doctrine as is fundamentalism, but in reaction against an over-optimistic view of man. The aftermath of the war brought disillusion with man and his potential for improvement. God, say the neo-orthodox, is far more transcendent and his ways past finding out than the liberals contended. Neo-orthodoxy is reason's repudiation of reason's ability to bring about the salvation of man and his society. It is no coincidence that liberalism today is far less alive in Europe than it is in America.

Neo-orthodoxy is Christian pessimism. Those who oppose it say it is a defeatist position; those who espouse it call it a realistic interpretation of human nature. Liberals accuse the movement of disfiguring the dignity of man. Others charge that God is placed so far above man that he can no longer work through man. Fundamentalists attack it because it did not grow out of a loyalty to an infallible Scripture and does not confine the concept of the Word of God to the Scripture. They charge the neo-orthodox with being liberals in orthodox clothing.

UNITY IN THE DOCTRINES OF THE CHURCH

The effect that each of these movements has had on the church stems as much from the critics as from the proponents. Even though these criticisms are often ably denied they continue to shape opinion. Any counseling with its theological anchor in one of these movements would antagonize the others. Those in these groups, however, belong to denominations with a theological heritage. Although this heritage shows denominational characteristics, these differences are not large enough to create any marked disunity in pastoral counseling.

Denominations are often called necessary evils, and some would deny their necessity. But the spirit of ecumenicity is not violated simply because there are denominations, so long as these denominations work with each other and not against each other. It is an encouraging fact that the old denominational antagonisms have largely subsided. Each group has made its own distinctive contribution to the enrichment of Christendom. This is particularly evident when we study confessional theology. The church is one in spite of denominations.

Some may feel that these doctrines of our heritage are retained more out of respect for the past than for their meaning today. The fact remains however that the denominations hold forth these doctrines as their official theological position. Furthermore when we relate these doctrines to pastoral counseling we shall allow them to prove their pertinence. In doing so I propose to interpret them according to the historical experience out of which they developed and not in terms of any of our current theological movements. If at any time this interpretation appears to reflect the position of one of these movements it will indicate only the nearness of this movement to the historical interpretation at that point.

We shall be dealing with a heritage that has had a great meaning for the counseling of the past and one which I believe has an even greater meaning for the counseling of today. Our challenge therefore is to incorporate the pastor's own heritage into pastoral counseling—to bolster its psychological framework with a theological foundation—to the strengthening of this personal ministry to people with problems.

At first glance these doctrines seem shallow in comparison with the theological treatises of the current schools of thought.

They were formulated for the layman as well as the clergy; they are brief and simple, but they are also clear and practical. Their profundity will be manifested more in their relation to the dynamics of personality than in quoting them from their historical context.

THE HISTORICAL DOCUMENTS

We find the theology of the church in the confessional documents of Christendom. These include the confessions from the period of the Reformation, such as the Augsburg Confession of the Lutheran Church, the Westminster Confession of the Presbyterian Church, the Heidelberg Catechism of the Reformed Churches and the Thirty-nine Articles of the Anglican and Protestant Episcopal Churches. These latter form the basis for the Articles of Religion in the Discipline of the Methodist Church. In a secondary sense theology is found also in the writings of the Reformers, such as Luther's *Treatise on Christian Liberty*, Calvin's *Institutes of the Christian Religion*, Zwingli's *Commentary on True and False Religion* and, later, Wesley's sermons. These Reformation creeds are joined with later confessions such as the New Hampshire Confession of the Baptists, the Kansas City Confession of the Congregationalists, and the Confession of Faith of the Evangelical United Brethren Church, a modification of the Methodist Articles of Religion. There are also doctrinal formulations in the writings of the founders of those denominations which have no creeds, such as Robert Barclay of the Society of Friends and Alexander Campbell of the Disciples of Christ. It is of interest to note that the age of creedal formulation is still going on. The present tendency toward denominational mergers has necessitated a fresh interest in new creeds, an example of which is the Creed of the United Church of Canada, a body of twenty articles of faith upon which the

Methodists, Congregationalists, and Presbyterians of Canada united in 1927. One of the latest of these creeds is the United Testimony on Faith and Life, formulated in 1952 by a delegated committee of laymen, pastors, and theologians as a basis for the proposed merger between four Lutheran churches.

These confessions are joined to the early church by the ecumenical creeds of eastern and western Christendom, the Apostles', Nicene, and Athanasian; by the theological dissertations of Augustine, whom Nichols calls the greatest figure in the church between Paul and Luther,[3] whose writings have had a major influence in the theological development of Roman Catholicism as well as the Lutheran and Calvinist wings of the Reformation; by the writings of the Ante- and Post-Nicene Fathers of the eastern and western areas of the church; and finally by the letters of the theologian of the Scriptures, Paul.

Although these confessions vary considerably in their length and scope, their content is more uniform and is usually systematized as follows:

1. The doctrine of God
2. The doctrine of creation and providence
3. The doctrine of man
    a. The doctrine of the image of God
    b. The doctrine of sin
4. The doctrine of the Person of Christ
5. The doctrine of redemption
6. The doctrine of the Holy Spirit
7. The doctrine of the means of grace
8. The doctrine of sanctification
9. The doctrine of Christian liberty
10. The doctrine of the church

[3] Robert H. Nichols, *The Growth of the Christian Church* (Philadelphia: Westminster, 1941), p. 58.

   a. The doctrine of the ministry
   b. The doctrine of the universal priesthood

11. The doctrine of the last things (eschatology)

Although these doctrines are obviously interrelated it is beyond our purpose to investigate each of them. Rather we shall limit ourselves to those doctrines that deal specifically with the inner life and relate directly to the counseling process. In theology these doctrines have their own peculiar terminology. Perhaps the continued usage of this terminology, emotionalized by a history of conflict and misunderstanding, is in itself a barrier between this heritage and pastoral counseling. The terminology of the psychology of personality, for example, is certainly different from the vocabulary in the doctrine of man, and yet when we reduce them both to common parlance we find we are dealing with essentially the same basic principles.

PLACE OF THEOLOGY IN RELIGION

Some may feel that bringing theology into pastoral counseling is encumbering it with excess baggage. The religion of pastoral counseling they say should be simple. It is enough to know that the Bible has some good thoughts in it; no need to get involved in the doctrine of inspiration or the means of grace. But if this is all that is needed in counseling, why is more needed in anything else pertaining to religion? What after all is the purpose of theology and what is its relationship to religion?

In this reduction of religion to its lowest common denominator, have we done to it what we did to bread? We took out all the rough stuff from the wheat to make our bread soft and fluffy. Then we discovered that we had taken out the vitamins. Now we put back what we took out and call it "enriched."

Theology gives structure to religion. It gives it body so that the intellect can share in the venture of faith. It tells the how and the why as well as the what. It is the solid stuff that lends character to religion and stability to the religious personality. Instead of uselessly complicating religion, it fortifies it. If theology "enriches" religion then it ought to contribute to the potency of religion to "enrich" the lives of people. It should therefore be a valuable tool in pastoral counseling.

In using client-centered methods pastoral counseling has had to fit them to religion or to fit religion to them and somewhere in the process theology has become a casualty. Client-centered therapy humbles the counselor. That is good. But it is not good to humble religion also in the process. In other words, while client-centered therapy can be used in pastoral counseling, it must not be allowed to gain at the expense of the theological heritage of the church.

Naturally if the counselee is the center of direction, the pastor's use of theology will be limited, but surely no more so than the secular counselor's use of the fundamentals of psychology. Both must restrain their impulse to point out where the principles of their specialty apply until the moment when the counselee sees the connection himself or at least is in a receptive frame of mind. Theology has a relationship to religion similar to that of psychology to human nature; they deal with much common ground, but from a different approach. Principles of psychology were known intuitively by the poets and prophets of the ages. Psychology has given to these principles a system of verbalization that has made them tools for scientific thinking. In a similar manner theology in its origin in revelation is both an expression of and a stimulus to religious experience.

Since the problems of personality have their origin more in the emotions than in the intellect it is obvious that the role of the intellect in psychotherapy is limited and can easily be overemphasized. It is also obvious that to ignore the intellect is a reaction in the other extreme. Any view of personality adequate in the therapeutic process must include the totality of personality. When a person is disturbed he is disturbed not only in a portion of his personality but in his entirety. Without minimizing the dangers of overintellectualization we can safely say that since the intellect is involved in the problem it can be a help in overcoming the problem providing its limited role is understood, even as the intellectual content of religion can be a help in the stimulation of religious experience, providing its role is not overemphasized at the expense of the other features of religion.

THEOLOGY AND DOGMATISM

Others may feel that bringing theology into the counseling process is a regression to dogmatism. Since the pastor has been guilty at times of using his theology as an evidence of his authority, theology has become associated with authoritarianism. Again the pastor has been known to give moral and religious advice that has created more problems than it has solved. Such advice is at least partially traceable to his personal theology; yet it brings discredit on theology itself. The pastor has failed as a counselor, it is charged, because he has functioned in a dogmatic way. The popularity of the client-centered approach in pastoral counseling as we have noted may be a reaction against this dogmatic attitude, which many hold responsible for the reluctance of the layman to talk over his problems with his pastor. If it is true that people are not going to their pastor with their problems—and I believe it is—then part of the blame falls on the pastor. If by a dogmatic attitude we mean an unwillingness or inability to understand human nature, the pastor who has it will drive his people away.

Opinionated, bigoted men who are given to quick judgments are not the kind to attract people with problems since they obviously have not faced their own problems. Dogmatism however is no more a part of our theological heritage than it is of any other mental discipline. Dogmatism is a frame of mind and can fashion itself around various ideologies. Dogmatic use of theology, or even worse, espousal of harmful theology, usually has its origin in a warped personality or society or both.

But are there enough pastors with this kind of attitude to account for the failure of the profession as counselors? Both charity and reason would say "no." The difficulty is with the pastor's ego. When someone comes to him with a problem he feels obligated to solve it. In his anxiety to fulfil what he feels is expected of him he may prematurely let go with his ideas and advice. This attitude of the pastor is also more a problem of psychology than of theology.

Many do not go to their pastor with their problems also because they are in the habit of keeping their problems to themselves. To seek help in these problems would be embarrassing, even humiliating, to them. Our culture has trained our people—especially our men—to conceal their tender emotions. It is no wonder that they hesitate to expose these feelings even to their pastor. If we had had a multitude of successful pastoral counselors in the past they might have broken through this shell around church people. Yet this speculation is of little value to the pastor of today. His job is not only that he be a capable counselor. He must also educate his people to come to him so that he can put his counseling to use.

Dr. Thorne, in his book, *Personality Counseling*, includes a section on pastoral counseling in which he says that "the validity of revealed truth would be tremendously strengthened if science could clarify some of the relationships involved." [4] We will attempt to follow Thorne's suggestion. We can hope that the comparison will be mutually profitable; that the clinical data on counseling will clarify our understanding of theological doctrines, and that these doctrines also will have their clarifying effect on the data. Thorne goes on to say:

> It must be recognized, however, that research evidence concerning the validity of spiritual approaches to counseling and psychotherapy is currently lacking and it remains to be demonstrated that pastoral counseling has developed any valid methods beyond those which are utilized in psychiatry and psychology.[5]

Could it be that if Thorne is correct—and as a whole I think he is—pastoral counseling missed its opportunity to contribute to the methods of psychiatry and psychology in its neglect of its theological heritage? This is the problem that I undertake to explore. My purpose is to correlate the data of the psychology of clinical research with our theological heritage for pastoral counseling. Whatever we shall accomplish in this manner will at least be a step in the direction of meeting the challenge that lies in Thorne's indictment.

[4] Frederick C. Thorne, *Principles of Personality Counseling* (Brandon, Vt.: Journal of Clinical Psychology, 1950), p. 482.
[5] *Ibid.*, p. 20.

CHAPTER TWO

The Need for a Listener

I shall endeavor first to develop the principles of counseling, together with an introduction to their correlation with theology, and follow this with a more concentrated study into theology, with specific application to the counseling method. My reason for this procedure is to correlate the theology of the church with pastoral counseling in a systematized manner resembling the familiar approach to the study of dogmatics. Each of the theological concepts involved is applicable to each of the counseling principles. To present these doctrines simultaneously with the principles of counseling would mean a redundancy that may reduce the clarity of the correlation. At the risk of appearing to compartmentalize the material—which is certainly not my intent since psychology and theology are united in their purpose—I believe the correlation can be most effectively demonstrated after we have understood the principles of the counseling process. Actually the pastor has two problems regarding his counseling ministry: how to get people to come to him with their problems[1] and what to do with them when they come. Although it may seem that we are getting the cart before the horse it is only the latter problem with which we are concerned in this book.

[1] For a discussion of this problem, see William E. Hulme, *How to Start Counseling* (Nashville: Abingdon, 1954).

The principles of counseling have grown out of the science of dynamic psychology and no discussion of them can separate itself from this background. Yet these principles can also be said to be native to pastoral counseling. As Allport has observed: "It would be difficult, I suspect, to find any proposition in modern mental hygiene that has not been expressed with venerable symbols in some portion of the world's religious literature."[2] The verbal garb is different; the observations the same. The origin is in man's common experience in dealing with the needs of troubled souls. Both theology and psychology are devoted to meeting these needs. Because of this I desire to present these principles in terms of the needs of people with the problems out of which they have developed. I have listed these needs as: (1) The need for a listener. (2) The need for confession. (3) The need for understanding. (4) The need for growth.

This division is primarily for the purpose of presenting the material and is not meant to be any unique analysis of the subject. These needs overlap in much the same way as do the doctrines of theology. Confession and understanding for example are not only a part of the growth process but require a certain amount of growth before they can occur. In fact we can list the growth of the counselee as the aim of the entire counseling process; the pastor's ultimate task is to minister not only to the justification but also to the sanctification of his parishioner. This same overlapping exists between the doctrines of justification and sanctification. Though they must retain their separate identities if they are to have any meaning, they are so interdependent that we cannot discuss the one without including the other. In addition the influence of

[2] Gordon W. Allport, *The Individual and His Religion* (New York: Macmillan, 1951), p. 86.

both is inseparable from the doctrines of the universal priesthood and Christian liberty.

Lest there be any misunderstanding, there is more to pastoral counseling than method—regardless of how sound from a psychological or theological point of view the principles are upon which the method is based. The pastoral counselor is a person and the counseling process can hardly be discussed apart from the personality of the counselor.[3] The pastor's spirit is the power behind the method. The warmth of his bearing, the sincerity of his intention, and the depth of his spirituality are traits that cannot be manufactured by methods; they are perceived in ways other than the spoken word. They and not the method make the pastor.

For this reason it is an impossible task to record the counseling process on paper. The examples of actual counseling interviews that will be used as illustrations (with fictitious names) were written from memory and not tape recorded. This limitation is minimized when we realize that even the tape recorder cannot capture the unspoken personal communications and reactions of the counseling process. And even the voice inflections that it does record cannot be duplicated in transmission to the printed page.

The method gives to the spirit wisdom. Yet the method can be used unwisely. There is always the danger of legalism in the use of any code of principles. As in the case of theological doctrines, the verbal formulations can become ends in themselves rather than means to an end, and as such become separated from the spirit of which the formulation was the symbol. Instead of being a method to improve the counseling process it becomes a hindrance to it. The pastor develops a mechanical attitude which not only prevents him from reacting spon-

[3] This is abundantly demonstrated in Hiltner's *The Counselor in Counseling.*

taneously to the peculiarities of the individual counselees and to unexpected developments in the counseling situation, but also undermines the confidence in the pastor of any counselee sensitive enough to be aware of it. A counseling method is simply the application of the principles of psychology and theology to one in need. When the psychology and theology are in harmony they will produce a similar method. When either psychology or theology are misused in a legalistic way, they no longer correspond to the inner dynamics of personality and procedures based upon either lose their efficacy.

There is of course the temporary danger of becoming legalistic with any method of operation during the learning process. Our goal as pastors is to use these principles in our counseling contacts until they become second nature to us. If we can relieve our minds of the necessity of remembering a method we can concentrate instead on the counselee as a person and allow the spirit of the method to prevail.

As one attempts to follow the principles of counseling he learns many things that he cannot learn out of books. He makes mistakes–plenty of them–and this is unfortunate for his parishioner. Yet in the providence of God his counseling may succeed in spite of his blunders. Even though we are acquainted with the principles of counseling it is often in our violation of these principles that we learn to appreciate them and to use them. In my record file I keep a card on which I write the things I learn the hard way. Every once in a while I look this list over to fortify my train of thought along these lines. I *knew* these things before I *learned* them. They are on my list now because they registered with me only after I had made enough mistakes–and seen the consequences of these mistakes–to realize their importance. The primary goal of the counselor is also to grow.

SOMEONE TO LISTEN

"So you give advice to the students." This is what people usually say when I tell them I am a pastoral counselor on a college campus. Although there may be a place for advice in the counseling process it is certainly on the periphery; there is a deeper meaning to counseling than that popularized by Mr. Anthony. In fact this type of problem-solving can scarcely be called counseling in the dynamic meaning of the word. Giving advice may miss the heart of the problem; it may also do harm. There are too many victims of poor advice and too few people who are wise enough to decide the course of other people's lives. The difficulty is with the word counsel: it *means* advice. Since the process of counseling is not primarily giving advice it seems we are in need of a more appropriate term by which to describe it.

Dissociating ourselves from the traditional interpretation of counseling we can say that the need for a counselor is first of all the need for someone to talk to. People with problems are literally filled up. In talking things over with a counselor they empty themselves and feel relieved. They may surprise the counselor by expressing extreme gratitude for his help. "I didn't really do anything," he may say, "I just listened." He can honestly be humble: simply by listening he has done a great deal. In line with the emphasis in the doctrine of the priesthood of the believer the counselee who has free access to God experiences this same release through prayer. God is a good listener.

I used to minister to a man who had been an invalid for years. As he neared the end of his struggle to live he said to me, "Pastor, when you are sick, you are sick alone." Sickness is one kind of problem. The person who has a problem, regardless of what it is, views it as a threat to his security. In his problem he feels alone. Let him find someone who will try to understand how he feels and he experiences the beginnings of a fellowship in the most isolated part of his life. The problem no longer seems so unbearable: someone in a small way is sharing it.

Although the need for a friend who listens and tries to understand is fundamental to counseling it is no new discovery. People with problems have known this is what they have wanted as long as people have had problems. Usually it is the *counselor* who needs to learn this fundamental. When a married student came to me with a serious financial problem, almost as a matter of course I began to seek for ways to relieve his situation. "Listen," he said, "I didn't come to you expecting you to solve my problem. I just wanted to talk to somebody about it—I want to get it off my chest."

The better pastors in all ages were men who knew how to listen. Although many lived before the emergence of psychology as a science, they were helped to this knowledge by the theological heritage which guided their thinking.

HOW TO LISTEN

Listening is a skill. It is not merely remaining silent while another speaks—although it is that of course. I recall a pastoral counseling demonstration where the pastor remained silent during the "interview"! His poor "counselee" had to do some fast thinking to keep the demonstration going. I am afraid in actual practice the counselee would have given up and concluded he may as well stay at home and talk to the wall. While listening may curtail the activity of the pastor it is nevertheless an active participation of the pastor in the counseling process. The fact that the counselor is a person and not a wall is the basis of the counseling process and he manifests his personality by taking a personal interest in the counselee and what he is saying. He shows this interest by responding in a clarifying way to the communication of the counselee. There is no *one* way of doing this. "Um-hmm" may suffice in one instance while a restatement of the communication of the counselee may be better in another, and a single nod of the head in still another. The disciplined and yet spontaneous insight of the pastor, judging each counseling relationship on its own merits, must be the determining influence, and not a stereotyped formula for response or even for a variety in response. As Emerson said, it is the spirit that teacheth, and so also it is the spirit that counsels. And as Louttit points out, even in the client-centered approach the counselor, by virtue of his status, exerts a very real directive influence whether he wants to or not.[4] The theological description of the relationship between the pastor and his counselee is one of love. Love may be disinterested in the sense of impartiality, but never in the sense of indifference, and it is certainly an influence the pastor projects into the counseling relationship.

Kenneth Baltus, a young man in his middle twenties, asked his pastor for an appointment. When he arrived there was the usual introductory "small talk" and then the pastor brought the counseling process to a beginning by saying:

PASTOR: Well, Kenneth, what's on your mind?

KENNETH: Oh, I've been doing a lot of thinking lately—about myself that is—and I decided I would like to talk to you. I think I've got a pretty big problem and it will take quite a while to go over it.

PASTOR: I see. Go right ahead. (The pastor indicates he understands and accepts these conditions. He gives the go-signal to Kenneth to express his problem.)

KENNETH: It is hard to know where to begin.

PASTOR: As you said, the problem is rather big and it is hard

[4] C. M. Louttit, *Clinical Psychology* (New York: Harper, 1947), p. 156.

to know where to get hold of it. Probably if you will just start anywhere you will come out at the same place. (He shows he understands a frequent predicament in getting started. His suggestion is an uncoercive attempt to aid Kenneth to express himself.)

KENNETH: I've always been what you would call "personality-conscious." I read every book on the subject. Yet I never feel that I'm "on the in" with others.

PASTOR: You don't feel your personality fits in well with others and you study a great deal to find out why. (The pastor does not tell Kenneth he understands but gives him instead the proof for it. At the same time he clarifies what Kenneth has said.)

KENNETH: Yes. It gets me down. I get into terrible moods and don't seem to be able to throw them off.

PASTOR: When you feel left out by others it depresses you. (Again he captures the feelings that were expressed and this demonstration of understanding and clarity encourages Kenneth to go on.)

KENNETH: That's it. It is getting so that I am about to break up with Pat. We are just not hitting it off. It isn't that we quarrel. She's moody too and together we are a couple of dead-beats.

PASTOR: Moodiness doesn't make for congenial dating, does it? (Here the pastor continues his understanding approach but varies it in tune with his personality.)

KENNETH: You can say that again. (He shows he appreciates the way the pastor is grasping his problem and the seriousness of it.) The trouble is—this has happened before. Am I going to be unable to find any lasting relationships with the opposite sex?

PASTOR: You are wondering if there is something about your personality that will continue to cause your relationships with a girl friend to break off after a certain length of time.

(By restating in different words what Kenneth himself expressed he sharpens the focus on this underlying fear. With the fear thus accepted Kenneth readily continues along this vein.)

KENNETH: That's it. After all it isn't too pleasant a thought. Like everybody else I would like to be married someday and have a family of my own. Probably all the more so with me since as you know I've never had what you would call a real home.

Caution must be taken that one restates only what the counselee expresses and not what we may think he alludes to. Suppose instead of his previous response the pastor would have said: "You are worried that you might end up not married." Although this may have been true Kenneth may not be willing to accept it coming from the counselor. Instead of the highly revealing comment he made he might have become defensive and said something like this: "It's not only that I am thinking about marriage." If the pastor gets ahead of his counselee in this manner his best procedure is to accept the protest of the counselee and gracefully retreat until the lost ground can be regained and he can be alert when the opportunity presents itself again. It is the position of the theology of the church that man is created as a free being and therefore as a responsible being. The pastor's listening approach is based on his respect for both of these qualities in his counselee.

LISTENING DIFFICULTIES

People differ in their readiness to express themselves. Those of a more taciturn disposition can be a source of frustration to a counselor. How can he listen to them when they do not talk? His challenge is to stimulate them to talk in a pump-priming sort of way. A gentle suggestion such as, "Would you like to tell me how you feel about it?" or "Can you recall how all this began?" may initiate a feeble flow of conversation to which the counselor can respond as in the above interview in an effort to maintain and increase the flow. However he must guard the process against the danger of degenerating into a question and answer type of communication. The counselee will feel like a patient in a physician's office describing where and how he hurts so that the physician can make the diagnosis and prescribe the remedy. Before he is aware of it the pastor may find himself taking over the responsibility for the problem and handing out advice. As we shall see in a later chapter, if the counselee is to grow he must retain the responsibility for his own problem.

Although he may think that he has an easier time listening to people who talk freely the pastor needs to remember that not all talk is helpful talk. The conversation of garrulous people though flowing freely is as often a defense mechanism to cover up the real problem as it is an expression of it. Although the taciturn speak with much less ease, their speech is usually of more significance to their problem. The pastor need not fear periods of silence in these relationships. Taciturn people are used to pauses in their conversations and it is not uncommon for them to break off these pauses with some very pertinent comment. They are usually shy people and will warm up in ensuing interviews as they become accustomed to the counseling relationship.

Probably the most difficult people to form a listening relationship with are those who analyze the counselor. They are usually young people who, having personality problems of their own, have taken to observing the operation of personality in others. Often quite sharp in noticing little irregularities they break into the listening process by questioning the intentions of the counselor and his motives in his comments and responses. To the pastor this may become aggravating since it tends to put him on the defensive. Actually these individuals are testing him out and though they have within them a diffuse sort of antagonism, they need the security of his close relationship. If he can accept their rather brash approach and bear with them in patience he will usually gain their confidence.

GETTING TO THE REAL PROBLEM

Skilled listening on the part of the pastor prevents the counseling process from becoming fixed on a sideline and never getting to the real problem. When an individual asks for an appointment the counselor naturally thinks the matter is important. When the individual states his problem, however, it may be quite trivial. The counselor may be disappointed and rather half-heartedly bring the interview to a close; or he may be relieved that the problem is nothing more and wind up the interview accordingly. In either case he has good possibilities of being duped. The counselee often sends up a trial balloon before he gets to his real purpose.

As I go over the records of my counseling relationships I am amazed at how many of these people came to see me on matters other than their problem. There was the lady who was having trouble with her mother-in-law. About halfway through the interview she was making confession of her past sins over which she had much guilt. When the session came to a close we were on the problem of her unhappy relationship with her husband. There was the freshman girl who tearfully lamented her poor grades. From her grades we went to her nervous tension and from this to her unhappy home life. Her anxiety over her wayward father was far more of a problem to her than her poor grades and was largely responsible for these grades. There was the middle-aged woman who tearfully lamented the poor job she thought she was doing as a

Sunday school teacher. She said she was so discouraged that she had almost quit on several occasions. She felt undeserving, she said, in having the class. This was later followed by the even more significant statement that God couldn't possibly bless her efforts. Within a half hour she was almost hysterically releasing her pent-up remorse over an abortion fifteen years before. When she left she was still bewildered over what had happened. "How did we ever get to this," she asked. "It isn't what I came to see you about, but I'm glad I finally talked to somebody about it."

People often bring religious questions to their pastor as an introduction to their problem. As an example of this, an exemplary Christian gentleman asked me in a casual way for my interpretation of the verse: "This do in remembrance of me." What he really wanted to know and what I found out after much discussion was whether there was any way out of his obligation to take communion. He had unresolved guilt feelings which he could not identify but which made partaking of the Lord's Supper a most unpleasant experience. Others come to talk with the pastor concerning the problems of somebody else. Often they end up discussing their own.

Why does the counselee make it so hard for the counselor? For one thing he is afraid. He knows he should see the counselor, but after he arrives he loses his nerve. Although he hopes to get help he also is hesitant to reveal his soul. Often he is ashamed of his problem. For six interviews I counseled with a youth concerning his problem of feeling inferior socially. I opened the seventh interview by saying:

PASTOR: Well, where would you like to begin today?

COUNSELEE: (After a pause of about thirty seconds) There is something I would like to get off my mind. I've been wanting to tell you for a long time but just couldn't.

PASTOR: Go ahead.

COUNSELEE: It's kind of hard to say. I have a bad habit. I–I masturbate. I didn't want to tell you. I was afraid of what you might think of me.

Here was the evidence of an underlying guilt extremely pertinent to his problem. He had been ashamed to mention it. A sensitive person would have to trust another before he would tell him information of this nature, and it takes an accumulation of positive results with the trial balloons to develop this trust.

Another reason for this delay is that the counselee is not always aware of his real problem. We learn from depth psychology that a person may repress what is too painful to remember. Although it is buried in the unconscious it continues to cause trouble in disguised ways. In the course of his listening the pastor encourages the counselee to reveal more and more of his inner life until the debris is unearthed and he becomes conscious of his real problem.

It should be obvious by this time that any intervention by the pastor of his own opinions or value judgments will not only interrupt the listening process but also the progress of the counseling—at least until he has arrived at the real problem. This is a particular hazard in marital counseling where the individual problems of the partners become projected into their relationship with each other. It usually takes considerable listening by the pastor before the partner who comes to him can see the role of his or her personality pattern in the immediate tension. While he can never be sure that he has gotten to all of the roots of the problem, the listening approach keeps the door open to going deeper if this is necessary. One can also transgress the listening process in the opposite direction and so press for the real problem that the counselee becomes fixed on the surface problem. It is wise to stay on a superficial level until the counselee begins to descend. If the pastor attempts to lead him to the depths he may stir up resistance and slow down rather than speed up the process.

When the young people's society president came to his pastor to talk over his decision to quit school and enlist in the armed services the pastor could see his mind was pretty well made up. As the counselee talked the pastor sensed that living under temporary draft deferments was getting on his nerves and that his desire to enlist was simply the desire to escape the uncertainty by taking the situation into his own hands. But he said nothing. Yet the young fellow broke into the counseling process to say, "Now don't tell me I'm trying to run away." The pastor was taken by surprise, wondering whether the boy was telepathic. "Why did you say that?" he said. "Because that's just what my dad's been trying to tell me and it isn't true."

The pastor still felt it was true. Because the father had gotten in too soon with his analysis, however, the resistance was too strong for the pastor to penetrate, even with the listening approach. So also the diagnostic questions or inferences on the part of the pastor may hit the nail on the head, but be ahead of the counselee and create more resistance than enlightenment.

THE PASTOR VS. LISTENING

In spite of the fact that the need for listening has been stressed considerably the pastor's most common fault as a counselor is his failure to meet this need. Undoubtedly this is due in part to the influence of the other functions of the office of the ministry. As a preacher and teacher he does the talking while others listen to him. In his administrative capacity he is continually called upon for his opinion. At social functions he is asked to "say a few words." Conditioned in this manner to a dominant role he is likely to follow this habit pattern in his counseling. The small but increasing number of pastors who have had clinical training in counseling stand out as exceptions to this tendency. The intensity of this program is sufficient to break up old habits and to form new ones.

There are also some psychological factors that make it hard for the pastor to listen. The counselee has no corner on insecurity: he simply has more of it at the moment than some others. The counselor also is no machine: he has an ego too. He is an individual with emotion as well as with intellect. Whatever insecurity he has within him comes to the surface in the counseling process.

Someone brings him a problem. Naturally this person considers him capable of doing something about the problem. The counselor feels this. Suppose he should disappoint this person! Perhaps he is an influential individual in the congregation or the community. If he can satisfy him it will probably mean a lot for his reputation as a counselor. Perhaps he is a critical individual, one who was skeptical about coming in the first place, one who is educated and analyzes the counselor. If the pastor is going to allow the counselee to solve his own problem he dare not become defensive of his position. Considering the conditions under which he counsels, however, this is easier said than done.

The pastoral counselor sees a great deal of sadness. He ministers to his people in the hour of grief and pain. He may have a reluctance to counsel with people in sorrow because he seems so fortunate in comparison. Many of those who have deep-seated personality problems have much resentment within them. The counselor can sense this resentment; he may even have to serve as a scapegoat for some of it. Others come to the pastor because somebody suggested it to them.

They may frankly tell him so and leave him with the feeling that he must justify this recommendation.

Counseling with people who have these types of problems can make the pastor a little uneasy. He feels the necessity of convincing them that he is capable of counseling with them. He must show the grief-stricken that he is actually suffering with them; he must please the resentful lest he add to their resentment; he must make good for the one who recommended him as a counselor. With all these demands upon him to prove himself, it is only human that he should wonder if he will be able to do it, and when he does he is entertaining a fear which he will project into the counseling process. He carries his own problem into the counseling relationship and it becomes a question whose problem he is really trying to solve.

Not all of the people in the parish who have problems come to the pastor. He hears about their difficulties in roundabout ways. Can he help but wonder why they did not come to him? Naturally he wants to be *in* on the problems of his people; so he goes to them. It is a different matter when the counselor goes to the people than when the people come to the counselor. Will they resent his coming? Will they resist his offer to help? In taking the initiative for the counseling relationship he may feel the need to justify his proposition by making sure that his counseling will be successful. It takes a strong faith in the principles of counseling not to grab the bull by the horns and, too apprehensive to listen with any skill, try to do for the counselee what the counselee should do for himself.

The only way to prevent this from happening is to reinforce the structure of his role in his own mind. He is offering a service to these people which they in all probability appreciate. His apprehensions over their feelings in regard to him are more the product of his own inferiority complex than of any critical attitude on their part. The counselee is usually too preoccupied with his own problem to put the counselor in the forefront of his attention.

When the counselor accepts the responsibility to solve the problem he will increase his portion of the conversation in the counseling interview. This is the danger sign because it means he is cutting down the conversation of the counselee. Only as the counselee is able to talk out his problem will he overcome it. Whatever interferes with the flow of his conversation is a monkey wrench in the machinery of the counseling process.

When the pastor uses these principles of counseling he will witness their value and will develop a faith in them. This faith is intensified when he understands these principles in terms of his theological heritage. The very finitude of himself as a human being and of psychology as a human science is enough to shake his confidence at critical moments. When his faith in his counseling procedure is associated with his faith in the Word of God, the realization of these human limitations is not so disturbing.

STRUCTURED AND YET UNHURRIED

As the counseling process unfolds it is evident that counseling is one activity that cannot be done in a hurry. The very nature of listening is a safeguard against manipulation of time on the part of the pastor. In this respect counseling remains a bulwark against the speed-up tempo of the modern world which has also entered the office of the ministry. People with problems usually have more than their share of tension; the atmosphere of the counseling interview should decrease rather than increase this tension. The speed-up tempo itself is responsible for much of this tension and must be kept out of the counseling relationship. The pastor however has a real challenge incorporating an activity that defies time into a schedule which is regulated by time.

Although the counseling interview should have a generous allotment of time it should also have its structural limits. A pastor worries enough about getting all of his duties accomplished without bringing these worries into the counseling relationship. If while he is listening to his counselee he is also anxious over how long the interview is going to continue, he is developing an inner tension of his own. Unconsciously he may glance at his watch and his counselee, hypersensitive as he is, begins to feel guilty over taking up so much time. He will probably mumble something about being sorry for bothering the pastor with his problem and the pastor, guilty over having given himself away, will assure him that he has plenty of time. The result is that the interview goes on and on until it goes stale.

When a person comes to his pastor with his problem it is usually best if the pastor will allocate in his mind about an hour for the interview. If the problem seems simple and he tries to dispose of it in short order, he is overlooking the possibility that the real problem has not yet come out. On the other hand the interview can be too long and thereby spoil its good effect. The time structure of an interview however cannot be an arbitrary one: there are exceptions to rules even as there are differences in people.

The ultimate aim of counseling is the growth of the counselee. The process of growth takes time and it often takes more than one interview to accomplish this purpose. After about an hour the counselor can suggest another interview in the near future. He may be pleasantly surprised to find in the next interview that his counselee is much improved. The several days between interviews were sufficient time to bring out the good effects of the previous session. Even though the counselor may feel that the problem has been solved in the initial interview, it is still advisable that he schedule a follow-up appointment. It takes a while to determine if a solution is really genuine. When the counselee's problem is deep-seated and of long standing he may have to see his counselor many times before he has the solution he desires.

The listening approach is simply the manifestation of the counselor's respect for the individual human personality. This is inherent in the doctrine of the priesthood of believers. No human being can function as an official mediator for another. In this new relationship Christ performs this function. It follows that in the counseling relationship the counselor may not "lord it over" the counselee. It is his responsibility to guide—by listening! This should set the pattern for man's relationship with man; man has something worth listening to—he has something to say. Those who infringe on the listening rights of others are violating the respect they owe to their own human family. These violators, even when they are counselors, may be lacking in respect for themselves.

SUMMARY

People with problems are usually those who have kept their problems to themselves. Before they need anything else they need to talk. This means that the counselor must learn to listen. People with problems have always been aware of their need for a listener. It is the pastor who has forgotten. The counseling process has put him on the defensive; he has become preoccupied with his own role. Feeling obligated to offer a solution, he is constrained to speak before he listens. As he counsels according to the principles of the art he develops an increasing faith in the workability of these principles. In the meantime he needs to remind himself again and again of the nature of his role in the counseling relationship.

The purpose of the counselor's response to what his counselee has said is to give him incentive to continue talking, to give him evidence that he has been understood, and to clarify what he has said so that he can continue in the direction of his real problem.

CHAPTER THREE

The Need for Confession

So far as the mechanics are concerned the need for confession is simply an extension of the need for a listener. Yet the role that confession plays in the therapeutic process makes it a distinct need among people with problems. Confession is an old word with a long history in religious usage. Its scientific counterpart is catharsis. There is however some flexibility in the use of the term, due in part to the difference between the Catholic and Protestant usage. Gordon Allport, for example, in discussing the limitations of the church confessional points out that only the confession of one's own sins is permitted. This prevents the counseling process from expanding into the environmental and interpersonal influences that are involved (the need for understanding). Since the confessor is not allowed to follow up these problems outside of the confessional, it is up to the parishioner to return for additional counseling. The complaint among the priests, says Allport, is that the parishioners do not do this.[1] Wise, on the other hand, would like to expand the confessional to include the entire counseling process. In fact he refers to his volume on pastoral counseling as a method for the hearing of confessions based on the scientific knowledge of personality.[2]

[1] Gordon W. Allport, *op. cit.*, p. 96.
[2] Carroll Wise, *op. cit.*, p. 156.

Our use of the term is in the more or less loosely historical sense of catharsis: the need for confession is the need on the part of the counselee to give expression to the guilt within him or to the other destructive emotions of anxiety and resentment which are usually associated with guilt. This does not mean that the counselee simply relates that he has these feelings, but that he actually releases these feelings in the presence of the counselor. Confession, therefore, is that part of the counseling process in which the counselee releases through self-expression the destructive emotions within him.

IMPORTANCE OF FEELINGS

What happens in a person's life is one thing; what effect this happening has in his life is another. It is the latter that concerns the counselor. The same thing can happen to two people and their reactions may be entirely different. Some people rise above obstacles, others beat their heads against them or lie prostrate before them.

Problems that are rational in character and can be solved with the needed information form a very small percentage of a counselor's cases. Usually the need for information is only the surface appearance of an otherwise emotionally imbedded problem. These are the destructive emotions that have been generated within the individual in reaction to the happenings without. Before the counselor can do any constructive work with his counselee he must discharge these destructive emotions.

Whenever the counselee gives some indication of his feelings in the matter he should be encouraged to keep talking. If the counselor shows by his response that he recognizes and understands the way his counselee feels or at least that he is willing to hear more about it, he is giving him the green light to continue in this vein. As we give expression to our negative feelings—particularly to one who is not emotionally involved in the problem—we often discharge them.

Mrs. Drake asked her pastor for an appointment after her marital discord had reached alarming proportions. The following is an excerpt from her first interview.

MRS. DRAKE: I'm afraid our marriage is breaking up. It's just one fight after another and I can't stand it any longer.

PASTOR: Things are in a pretty bad shape. (The pastor responds to the negative expressed.)

MRS. DRAKE: They couldn't be any worse. He's a devil, that's all there is to it. He's mean and nasty—especially when he has drink in him, and that's getting to be about half of the time.

PASTOR: Hm. (A variation in response that simply shows that the counselor is following with interest.)

MRS. DRAKE: He always wants his own way—especially in sex—ooh! Sometimes I think I hate him. (At this point her emotions lost all restraint and she sobbed bitterly.)

PASTOR: (after a pause) His behavior is repulsive to you. (Again he captures the negative with no attempt to enlarge or diminish.)

MRS. DRAKE: He can't love me. He just can't. He even threatens to strike me. I think he would too.

PASTOR: It seems to you that he couldn't love you and still treat you this way. (The pastor helps Mrs. Drake to release her resentment without becoming allied with her against her husband. It is very important that he retain his sympathetic objectivity; otherwise he will not help her to see deeper into the problem nor will he be available to Mr. Drake. Nor did he interrupt the catharsis to ask Mrs. Drake where she herself might be to blame.)

The next interview brought a change in the emotion released, as the following excerpt shows:

MRS. DRAKE: I think the trouble with him is he's never had to take responsibility.

PASTOR: Oh. And you feel this is part of the problem.

MRS. DRAKE: I think so. You know—I wonder—well, whether I always use the right approach with him. He isn't the easiest man to understand, you know.

PASTOR: You mean you may not handle this weakness of his the right way.

MRS. DRAKE: I have a temper myself, I'll have to admit. I suppose I say things that I shouldn't at times. Probably rubs him the wrong way.

Having released the predominant pressure of resentment Mrs. Drake is able now to express her guilt. This confession will have its effect on her future conduct in her marriage and in turn on her marriage. For when one of the partners reduces his role in the irritation, even if he is the less offending partner, it is very likely to have a positive influence upon the other. We will take up this whole question of insight and understanding in the next chapter.

Discharging negative feelings may not always be accomplished as readily as we would like. Many people complicate their problems by refusing to admit to themselves that they have these feelings. Religious people are often guilty of this practice; they know they are not supposed to envy, to resent, to fear or to grow discouraged, and their conscience may be unmerciful when they do. It is more livable therefore to rationalize or to deny these feelings than to acknowledge them—to sacrifice honesty for peace. The trouble is that it does not work. It is like ignoring a cold until it turns into pneumonia. Just because one tries to bury his destructive emotions does not mean they are dead. Instead of staying buried they return under a disguise and become more of a problem than before. Even worse, the person has initiated a pattern of dishonesty with himself that is an additional barrier to overcoming his problem. All of this is enforced by the conscience which carries the authority of the deity to the individual. The moralistic emphasis is anathema to both psychotherapy and the theology of the church, and it is to the release from its bondage that both are directed. The Christian means of acceptance, otherwise known as the gospel, liberates the individual from the captivity to his dated conscience, which, though it may have served some homeostatic purpose in its incipiency, is now a block to religious and personality maturity.

Since the act of repression is for such people a means of self-defense, it is obvious that they will resist any attempt to make them face their real feelings. It is like pulling the props out from the support of a badly sagging wall. Since such an attempt is a threat to what little security they have, they may even attack the counselor as a means of defending themselves. To further complicate the confession of their destructive emotions these people often adopt self-atoning compensations and rituals with which to keep their repressions in check. These activities may seem altruistic or even reverent in nature. The individuals themselves may convince themselves—again as a seal of defense—that their motives are obedience to God and concern for people.

As an example, Mrs. Vernon Baylor, a well-to-do woman in her late thirties, had been going to physicians for years for her nerves. While of late the scope of her worries had greatly expanded, originally her concern was for her young son. She had made it a practice to accompany him to and from school. Only under the stress of circumstances would she permit him to leave the home without her. And then she worried continually until he returned for fear something would happen to him. To Mrs. Baylor this unusual concern was a manifestation of her motherly duties. Actually it was the result of her own guilt feelings.

Her boy was the result of an unexpected and unwanted pregnancy. A religious woman with a tyrannical conscience, she could not bear to face the fact that she had ambivalent feelings toward the child: she both wanted him and did not want him. Because she was afraid something might happen to the boy she had no peace unless she was with him. Repressed was the fear that God would punish her for her resentful thoughts toward the child by allowing something to happen to the child. Mrs. Baylor had adopted a method of protecting herself from her repression which was becoming increasingly difficult to maintain. The result was an increasing disintegration of mind and body.

If Mrs. Baylor comes to her pastor with her problem he will do more harm than good if he tries to get her to confess to guilt feelings over her boy. She will be horrified that he even intimates such a thing—even though her actions have long intimated such a thing to him. She may transfer her anxiety to this incident and become all upset over it. Even worse her relationship with the pastor will probably be closed to further counseling.

It could well be that Mrs. Baylor's neurosis is so deep-seated and of such long standing that she needs more extensive therapy than counseling. Nevertheless if the pastor uses the listening approach in his counseling he will help her. In regard to her need for confession he should be alert to respond to any indication she may give of the presence of destructive emotions. In this manner he will encourage her to go further in this direction without taking the lead from her. The growth that she may experience in a relationship of this nature may enable her to release much of her negative feeling even though she may never reach the major repression. As a result her agitation may subside to the extent that she may learn to live a more or less normal life within acknowledged limitations.

REPENTANCE AND FORGIVENESS

Confession occupies a prominent role in the religious concept of repentance: before the sinner can receive the forgiveness of his sin he must repent of his sin. Repentance is the frame of mind that is receptive to this forgiveness. In addition to confession it includes a hope for forgiveness and a desire to overcome sin. People with problems are often blocked in this reception of forgiveness; in fact part of their problem is that they do not feel accepted or forgiven. God may be willing to forgive but man may be unable to allow Him. It is a problem in repentance. By means of the spoken Word, the counselor is to create the frame of mind within the counselee that will enable him to receive divine grace. Since this is the work ascribed to the Holy Spirit in the theology of the church, pastoral counseling can be considered a specific and chosen means by which the Holy Spirit accomplishes his work.

Our trouble comes about when our capacity for loving turns inward upon ourselves and becomes pride. This hinders our relationship with God. Before restoration of this relationship is possible the destructive emotions associated with pride need to be expressed. According to the doctrine of justification this catharsis is in preparation for the experience of acceptance which consummates the restoration. The entire experience is described by the psalmist:

> When I declared not my sin, my body wasted away
> through my groaning all day long.
> For day and night thy hand was heavy upon me;
> my strength was dried up as by the heat of summer.

I acknowledged my sin to thee,
and I did not hide my iniquity;
I said, "I will confess my transgressions to the Lord";
Then thou didst forgive the guilt of my sin.[3]

Once the confession takes place the resources for affecting the restoration are summed up in Christianity's gospel. As a minister of this gospel, the pastor can use this unique opportunity to make it good news for his troubled counselee.

Yet it is precisely at this point that the pastor often gums up the works.

He halts the flow of catharsis by an attempt to give reassurance. One can be too quick to pronounce the absolution. The confession not only brings to the consciousness of the counselee the full impact of his sin and hence of his need for forgiveness, but also effects the release of destructive emotions which otherwise form a blockage to any full reception of acceptance. Perhaps his reason for prematurely giving reassurance is that he cannot bear to see suffering. Anybody who has witnessed people going through the throes of guilt or fear knows how heart-rending this can be. Yet this very suffering can be redemptive: if it is allowed to run its course it will make the assurance of forgiveness all the more effective. Actually the pastor who is allergic to suffering is not acting out of love for the counselee. God for example shows love by allowing his people to suffer if by that suffering he can give them something greater in return. This is the meaning of the biblical concept of chastening and is an integral part of the doctrine of sanctification. The pastor's motive may be more of weakness and his reassurance more for himself than his counselee. The advent of God in Jesus Christ is a manifestation of God's self-giving for man; the suffering of the

[3] Psalm 32:3-5.

Son is indicative of the sacrifice of the Father to fulfil the demands of his love to redeem his creation.

The pastor may interfere with the confession of his counselee with an even more dangerous type of reassurance than premature absolution, namely, by attempting to minimize the validity of the counselee's negative feelings, particularly his guilt. "I think you are taking this thing entirely too seriously," he may say, or "There is really nothing wrong in what you have done and so you just forget about it." While he may honestly hope to reduce the guilt by minimizing its cause, he may only succeed in demonstrating to the counselee that he does not understand how the counselee feels. He is going counter to the principles of both the science of sociology and the doctrine of Christian liberty, both of which point out that individual or group standards determine to some extent the nature of what is right or wrong for the individual. In matters of adiaphora Christian may differ with Christian. In the words of St. Paul: "I know and am persuaded in the Lord Jesus that nothing is unclean in itself: but it is unclean for anyone who thinks it unclean."[4] The doctrine of Christian liberty recognizes a legitimate relevancy to guilt, but a relevancy that is absolute to the individual. This "absolute conception of the relative" must be respected, according to this doctrine, if individuality is to be respected. Applied to pastoral counseling this conception gives us a method that leads to the emancipation of the conscience from the condemnation by law, to make possible its growth in being ruled by love.

What is needed is that the pastor should accept the counselee's confession of guilt regardless of how it disagrees with his own particular feelings. In the course of the counseling relationship the counselee himself may grow to question his conscience on these matters, providing the counselor accepts

[4] Romans 14:14.

his confession and allows it to go on. In the meantime the pastor should deal with the counselee where he is and not where he thinks he should be. This does not mean that factual information—as in masturbation for instance—cannot be given; it does mean that the counselee's guilt over masturbation is not resolved by any pooh-poohing of the seriousness of masturbation by the pastor. Even in those instances where the confession of guilt is obviously exaggerated beyond all cause or even appears irrational, the pastor will go further toward alleviating this guilt if he recognizes the neurotic nature of his counselee and accepts the confession as it is given. It is the motif of Christian theology that guilt results when an individual feels that because of his behavior he has separated himself from his Creator, whether he intellectually recognizes a Creator or not; and that guilt is removed only by the experience of divine forgiveness and never by explaining it away.

The content of confession is frequently of an intimate nature. To a sensitive counselee it is somewhat of a shock to realize that the pastor knows something about him that he probably hoped to keep to himself. The pastor is not like a secular counselor who passes out of one's life at the close of the counseling relationship. Instead he and the counselee may continue to rub shoulders in many different roles in the days ahead. Consequently the pastor is a constant reminder to the counselee that somebody else knows. Therefore it is very important that the pastor give every evidence both during and after the counseling relationship that he accepts the counselee as he is—that his secret sins and shames in no way influence the pastor's opinion of him or his worth.

THINGS WE DO NOT WANT TO HEAR

The same insecurity that causes the pastor to be defensive in his role as a counselor can also cause him to pass over things he does not want to hear. The clue to negative feelings which the counselee may drop may incite negative feelings also within the counselor. A young man for example in counseling with his pastor concerning his problem of indecision and lack of confidence, may allude to the fact that he has not always been what he should be in his relationship to women. The pastor may not want to hear this. If this boy to whom he has been pastor has fallen into the sin of fornication he may take it as a personal failure. Also to follow up such a remark would tend to enlarge the problem and he may feel more comfortable in keeping it as simple as he can. It may be easier in every way to ignore the hint and steer clear of it in his response.

Commonly it happens that a person having problems of doubt may be hesitant to state his problem flatly and may instead throw out a hint to his pastor that all is not well with his faith. Since the pastor knows that he and the faith are inseparably bound together to many of his people, he may see in such hints a threat to his own position. It gives him an uneasy feeling to think that any of his flock might be questioning his religion. And so he may pass off such allusions with a pious and often trite generality, such as, "We all go through these things occasionally." In both of these instances the pastor's own counterreaction to the indications of the need for confession will stifle the confession.

If the counselee in the course of his confession gives vent to feelings about things in which the pastor is emotionally involved, he may not merely pass over them, but rise up to refute them. If in giving expression to her feelings of rejection a young lady makes a caustic criticism of the young people's society, which the pastor feels is "his baby," he may attempt to show her—perhaps by cross examination tactics and all the while with his blood pressure going up—that the young people's society is innocent of any blame. Of course he stops the confession cold. Countercatharsis such as this on the part of the pastor is comparable to the injection of his own directions into the counseling process so that the counselee is ultimately hindered from growing.

The pastor's desire to make things look good may also cause him to oversimplify the problem. In trying to put his counselee at ease he identifies his problem with some general difficulty that most people pass through. To the counselee, however, his generalization may sound like a minimization. His problem he feels is unique, and not to be identified with even the similar cases the counselor may relate. Whether the counselor is right or wrong in his understanding of the problem his counselee will feel he is wrong and that he does not understand him. This raises a barrier between them that hinders the efficiency of the relationship.

The counselor's desire to see improvement can lead him to see more improvement than is actually present. The counselee may be unable to see where he has improved to this extent and feel that either the counselor is trying to pep him up at the expense of the truth or that he is incapable of understanding the real nature of the problem. For this reason it is normally a good procedure to allow him to make his own observations concerning his improvement. From a theological point of view this means that the counselor will allow himself to be governed by Christian liberty according to which one must be courageous enough to face the worst if he is ever to change it for the better.

People generally like to talk about themselves and the counselor is no exception. Listening to people describe their problems brings to his mind his own experiences with similar problems and he is tempted to tell about these in the interview. To the counselee the counselor is not just another person: he is one whom he respects. Consequently he may not see the similarity between himself and the counselor that the counselor points out. Perhaps this is fortunate because such an insight could cause a conflict in his mind over his counselor. It may seem incongruous to him that his pastor could have been contaminated with similar feelings. After he has overcome his problem to some extent he can better accept the weaknesses of others because he can better accept himself.

The pastor may so successfully overcome his reluctance to hear the clues to negative feelings that he no longer "hears" the expression of positive feelings. Their sound may even irritate him since he considers them a hindrance to getting to the bottom of the problem. Positive feelings however must also be accepted since they are a part of the counselee's communication of his inner self. A man may be lamenting to his pastor that he and his wife do not get along well together but may also add from time to time that things are better than they used to be. If the pastor ignores this expression of positive feelings, the man may think that the pastor believes things are worse than they really are, and in turn may break off his confession in order to re-emphasize this brighter side.

THE RESENTFUL AND THE MOODY

The individuals who can prove most exasperating to the pastor in meeting their need of confession are those whose release of resentment is scapegoated to the pastor and those whose resentment has spilled over into a mood of depression.

The Resentful. While most people have within them some measure of resentment these individuals can almost be characterized by this destructive emotion. There is nothing inadvertent about their remarks that sting the pastor: theirs is a direct attack. The danger is that the pastor may allow his ego to get involved in these emotional discharges and thereby lose his sense of objectivity. Even if he manages to refrain from any counteroffense or even defense, the jolt in itself may throw him off balance so that he forgets how to listen. If he can learn to roll with the punch he may be able to stay with the irascible until their emotional discharge has spent itself.

Ann Benson was a young woman who failed to make any satisfactory adjustment to those of her own social set and as a result was becoming bitter and antisocial. She did not belong to any church and was encouraged to see the pastor by a neighbor lady who belonged to the church. The neighbor also briefed the pastor and subsequently an interview was arranged. The prelude to her discharge of resentment against the pastor was her description of an ordeal at evening school.

ANN: Professor Samuels says I will get used to giving reports in class if I do it often enough. But I don't think so. Every time I give a report I make a fool out of myself. Then it is even harder to do the next time. I hate the class anyhow—it is full of those athletes.

PASTOR: You don't like to be in a class with athletes.

ANN: No. I don't like to be around boys. I've heard so many stories about them—I guess I am afraid of them. But if it wasn't this report it would be something else. I am always worrying about something. How am I going to get over these things?

This is one of those direct questions that demand quick thinking of the pastor. If he is to continue the listening approach he needs to keep the initiative with Ann by saying something like this: "You feel the need of overcoming this pattern of worry." Or, "Even though you get over one ordeal there is always another to take its place." The pastor however remembered that the neighbor lady had told him that Ann had no faith in anything or anybody, including God. He thought this was an opportunity to bring in religion.

PASTOR: How do you feel about religion as a help?

ANN: I used to pray, but it didn't do any good, so I quit. I think religion is for peasants. I can't see where anybody with intelligence could believe in it. God is somebody people invent to help them because they aren't strong enough to be alone.

PASTOR: I see.

ANN: Do you get credit for converting people who come to you or something? (The tone of her voice revealed more sarcasm than curiosity.)

PASTOR: Not at all. Religion is a help that I am sold on, that's all. (Realizing that he got more than he bargained for, the pastor tries to prevent the resentment from growing. His role is changing from that of listening to that of defending.)

ANN: I can't believe that! People don't really practice Christianity. I can't see any good in going to church. Those people in church! Ugh!

PASTOR: As you have brought out, your trouble is in your relationship with people. You do not feel close to anybody. Religion is a way of getting this feeling of security that you lack in not being close to anybody. (He tries hard to show her the wisdom of his position, but his appeal to reason is unable to influence her emotional reaction.)

ANN: Religion is *your* way!

PASTOR: OK, we will skip religion. I notice our time is about up. If you would like to come back again we will try something else. (Since the interview is now obviously an argument, the pastor bows out. He realizes that his defensive position is poor counseling but is still not able to get back on the listening track. Although his remark about the time being up was occasioned by the knock of his next appointment, it was still an escape. His listening approach is so shattered that he even structures the next interview on a "Mr. Anthony" basis.)

The Moody. The mood is the result of an accumulation of negative feelings brought on by the lack of any outlet for these feelings. Consequently the moody are in great need for confession. They pose a problem for the pastor when they arrive for their appointment in the throes of such a mood. Since it is one of the symptoms of a mood that the individual prefers not to talk and to be by himself, it is a challenge to stimulate the listening approach. Although a person in a mood appears devoid of emotion he is inwardly in agitation. In cases of acute depression the dominant emotion is anxiety. Individuals in this advanced stage of disintegration are usually in need of deeper therapy than counseling. The more common mood cycle is less severe and of shorter duration. The inner agitation of people in these moods is primarily resentment, often against oneself. In a counseling situation they can be irritating as well as frustrating to the counselor.

To the pastor an individual in a mood may appear intoxicated with indifference. He will admit anything bad about himself but in a disgustingly unco-operative way; he says he is disgusted with himself but in a manner that suggests inward defiance; he is unperturbed by long periods of silence as though he were sabotaging the interview; he seems unenthusiastic about the counseling relationship and consigns himself somewhat cynically to defeat; his remarks may seem to have barbs on them even though the literal wording is innocent. There is plenty of expression of negative feeling, but it does not appear to give any release; the pastor's responses which usually stimulate him to further communication seem scarcely to register. In short he acts as though he does not care. He may even yawn without embarrassment and glance at his watch as though he were wasting both his and the counselor's time.

The pastor may honestly wonder whether it is advisable to conduct the interview under such circumstances. The counselee usually realizes he is being unco-operative and afterward may feel guilty about it. He may apologize at his next interview or he may never return. Yet it is possible that the counseling interview could be the means for snapping him out of his mood—particularly if the pastor persists in the listening approach. The danger is that the pastor may resent this attitude and become as stubborn as the counselee. If *he* doesn't care, he may say, I'm sure *I* don't. It would be a shame if the decision to discontinue the interview were made under such circumstances. If the pastor understands the nature of the mood he can with practice retain his sense of objectivity so that he can with patience attempt to maintain a listening approach. While he may not feel he is getting anywhere he may be making gains which will show up when the mood lifts.

A knowledge of dynamic psychology in itself is no guarantee that the pastor can remain objective in his counseling. In fact this very knowledge furnishes him with a modern weapon with which to club the openly resentful or moodily resistant into co-operation. He may think he is responding to the feelings expressed but he does so with a vengeance. Because he is irritated he uses both his knowledge of psychology and counseling to show the counselee how stupid he is acting. He attempts to show his mastery of the situation by analyzing the counselee's actions. The unco-operative or antagonistic attitude of the counselee is a threat to his security at the moment, and his analysis of the counselee's behavior is an aggressive means to regain this security. The counselee however is already feeling inferior and only resents the pastor's attempt to show his superiority. As a result he becomes even more moody because he feels even more inferior and helpless. The pastor may use his theological understanding in this same vindictive manner. Whenever he uses the Christian message with a vengeance, in its psychological or theological setting, he has distorted it into a legalism. The only guarantee of the pastor's objectivity is his own maturity. Knowledge in itself will not give him this. If he uses this knowledge to understand himself better and to solve his own problems he will feel less threatened by the subtle or open hostility of his counselee.

There is another and less emotional way in which our attempts to analyze can interrupt the process of confession. As our counselee is talking we may be working ahead or behind in our minds in an attempt to piece together the fragments into a coherent whole. In the meantime we may be missing the clues to negative feelings. While it gives us a sense of control to have an explanation for things as we go along, it can also cause us to become mentally preoccupied with this figuring-out process when we should be alert to what is being communicated in words or actions at the moment. There is a need for understanding, but it is more the counselee's need than ours. And it must never interfere with the need for confession if its own requirements are to be satisfied.

SUMMARY

It is rare when a pastor can dismiss his counselee with some needed bit of information. Most problems that come to the pastor have their origin in the emotions rather than in the intellect. The dark powers behind the problems are the feelings of guilt, anxiety, and resentment which undermine the unity of personality and produce all manner of conflicts, sufferings, and failures. Because these feelings are negative and destructive, the counselee may try to bury them in the deep places of his inner life. Though buried they do not die but emerge in disguise to create even more disturbance than before.

Obviously we must discharge these negative powers before we can solve the problem. This is done by giving expression to them in the counseling relationship—by confessing them. The pastor facilitates this confession by his skill in responsive listening. After the counselee has talked out these feelings with his pastor he may discover that his tension has diminished and that he is more able to handle his problem than before. Where the problem is of long standing this improvement is not nearly so rapid and may require many sessions before it can be attained.

CHAPTER FOUR

The Need for Understanding

We fear that which we do not understand.

A person with problems usually has difficulty in understanding himself. The manner in which his inner life operates is a stimulus for all kinds of phobias and inner anxieties. Whatever appears to be irrational in an individual's understanding of his life situation undermines his sense of security. He feels unable to cope with his problems and lives in fear of life itself. To overcome his problem the counselee needs to understand it in terms of himself and others involved.

The greatest threat to a belief in God from a philosophical point of view is the problem of evil. Belief in a rational universe governed by a good God seems inharmonious with the presence of evil in this universe. So also the presence of evil in people's lives is a source of bewilderment to them and hinders their understanding of themselves and of the world about them. They need this understanding however so that they can handle their problems. So long as one keeps his problems to himself he is unlikely to get this understanding. Because his problem is actually a part of him and his reason is influenced by his emotions, he can no more see himself and his situation objectively than he can stand off and look at himself. To make it even more difficult his problem often has its roots in his attempt to escape from seeing things as they really are. According to the doctrine of man, evil creates this conflict, because it operates in violent contradiction to the image of God. Man cannot abandon himself completely to evil because he can never fully destroy the influence of this original righteousness.

In the counselee's initial condition of confusion it is obvious that he may not recognize the value of any explanation of his problem that his counselor may give him. His enlightenment must begin within him. If it comes from outside of him—even though it is the explanation he would have deduced himself—he may resist it. If the counselor tries to convince him that his interpretation is correct, he may grow defensive, feeling even that the counselor does not understand him, and the future of their relationship is endangered. In spite of all this effort by the counselor his counselee still does not understand.

To understand his problem he must get it out from inside of him and lay it on the table where he can take a look at it. He can do this by talking about it to a counselor. As he expresses his feelings through the medium of conversation he is transferring his problem to the outside. He often is surprised at some of the things he says as he realizes that he had not thought of things in this way before. He is developing new insights into the nature of his problem by objectifying it through expressing himself. The pastor accepts these developing insights even though he may not feel they are adequate. Perhaps they are not. But by accepting them he encourages the understanding process to continue so that more adequate insights may be attained. Should he attempt to correct or to argue or even to expand the insight he may inject a block into this growing understanding by undermining the counselee's confidence in his growing ability to understand or by stimulating a defensive reaction.

AREAS FOR EXPLORATION

During my first year in the pastorate one of my members brought to see me a nineteen-year-old boy who was in a state of acute depression. Bill, as we will call him, felt relieved after he talked with me, but in a few hours his anxiety and despair returned. During our interviews he could describe how he felt but he could not understand what was responsible for his condition. He was extremely fearful that he would not come out of it and would go insane. He was also afraid that he would take his own life.

Feeling that he needed deeper therapy than counseling I took him to a psychiatric clinic. After he had talked with Bill the psychiatrist suggested that in addition to his own work with him, Bill should continue his interviews with me. After about two weeks he showed definite signs of improvement and the psychiatrist called me in for a consultation. He explained that Bill's problem was centered in his relationship with his parents and aggravated by his relationship with his girl friend. What impressed me was not so much his diagnosis but that he had been able in such a short time to get this boy to relate all this significant information. In his interviews with me Bill spoke of these insights as his own. Furthermore he seemed to profit from this understanding.

The influences within the home in the early years of life shape personality. I knew this: I had read it many times in psychology books. Before that I had been taught it in religious instruction as the conclusion to the study of the moral law—visiting the iniquity of the fathers upon the children unto the third and fourth generation of them that hate me. It took this experience with the psychiatrist to bring home to me its practical application for the counselor. Christian theology maintains that those who yield to the influence of pride are unable to give the right kind of love to their children. Regardless of the heredity factor in original sin, its development is indebted to this sympathetic environment.

This influence of the home centers in the relationships the child has with the individuals within the home—father, mother, brother, sister. The quality of these relationships helps to create the personality pattern the child will take with him into adulthood. The many adjustments that an individual is called upon to make bring out the character of this pattern; they also bring on the problems.

The college campus offers an excellent demonstration of this connection between personality problems and these relationships of the past. The beginning student, away from home perhaps for the first time, is faced with the necessity of creating a new home. To do this he must win his place in a college family in which there is terrific competition for social recognition. Adjusting to those of his own sex is difficult enough but gaining the approval of those of the opposite sex is even more competitive. Since the date is the number one social pursuit on any coeducational campus the student feels it not only desirable but imperative that he participate. If in his own estimation he should fail to win the social recognition he desires, his disappointment is extremely painful.

He also faces the necessity to succeed in his intellectual pursuits. Here also his competition is strong. Should he be unable to compare favorably with his classmates he takes it as a reflection on his native intelligence. His loss of confidence in himself leaves him open to still further failure.

There are also those who do well in their grades but who allow this achievement to compensate for their failure in their social adjustment. Because they so desperately need good grades both as an escape from their social deficiencies and as a means for maintaining their self-respect, they want not only good grades but the best grades. Yet even a perfect score fails to bring satisfaction because they fear they will not be able to maintain it.

The personality pattern that the student brought with him out of his home background has a great deal to do with how he stands up to the demands of campus life and also how success or failure in meeting these demands will affect him. The student who develops no close friendships at college is more than likely to have had no acceptive relationship with his parents. Lack of acceptance is shown by overprotection and solicitude as well as by neglect and open rejection. With the latter he may be susceptible to moods, for he has had no one with whom to confide. His destructive emotions follow the pattern of piling up until they reach the needed intensity to spill over into a mood. If his parents did not give him the love and affection he needed, he may be unable to show love to others and as a result gives the impression of being cold and aloof. In the case of overprotection the student may draw back from the rough and tumble of the social milieu that shows so little appreciation of his person. The solicitous attitude betrays the parent's lack of confidence in the child, which attacks the child's own confidence when he faces any threat. Neglect and overprotection are distortions of love. Both psychotherapy and theology agree that the only influence that encourages people to grow is the reception of *agape*, genuine love. It is the presence of *agape*, both received and returned, that constitutes the theological motif of sanctification.

The role the student has had in his family group, the rivalries of brother and sister relationships, the attitude of his parents toward his creative abilities, all have their influence on his initiative. The student who has a lot of confidence in himself usually has parents who take an interest in him and encourage him, and those who withdraw in defeat before the challenges of college life have had their spirit dented in their formative years. People who have an excessive amount of inner tension can often find the origin of this tension in resentment arising out of the past and particularly out of the home. The student with a history of resentment against his parents may be quite aggressive, even belligerent—unscrupulous in seeking his ends and rationalizing his failures by blaming others. The opposite can also happen. He may develop strong feelings of guilt over his resentment and as a result of this conflict become a fearful and submissive person.

Although these earliest relationships within his home are the basis for an individual's pattern of destructive emotions, the relationships he has in the present also play a part in his problems. Of these the marital relationship is the most important. In marriage, husband and wife each give of themselves to the union of the two. Marriage therefore is the epitome of the close relationship, with all of its potential for the growth of personality. Yet for those who enter this estate and are not mature enough to adjust to such a partnership, marriage aggravates the weaknesses in their personalities and becomes an irritating factor in their problems. Much of the neurotic behavior of men and women that is so disruptive to the harmony of the group, such as the congregation or its societies, is due to the emotional chaos that results from the frustrating experience of an unsatisfying or querulous marital relationship.

A person's friendships—or lack of them—can also be a factor in his problems. Any close relationship leaves its mark on the personality. Usually a friendship is a good thing. Those without friends leave unsatisfied an important need of their personalities. For young people loneliness is extreme misery and a very serious problem. Older people may learn through the years to rationalize this emptiness by talking themselves into believing they are better off alone. One can have a friendship with an individual, however, whose personality is more of an influence for immaturity than for growth. One who is submissive may find friendship with an aggressive person. Each may be using the other to fill a need in their personalities by perpetuating their respective immaturities. Of greater moment are friendships between individuals of aggressive and submissive homosexual tendencies. Problems of such individuals are aggravated by these friendships.

Another trouble spot that the counselor should keep his eye on is the counselee's occupational situation. The American idea of success puts pressure on a man's ego. If he is not promoted he is frustrated and resentful: if he is, he faces the jealousy of his fellow workers. Who is getting a better deal and why? Am I marking time in this office? Is this the wrong job to make any money? Am I in with the boss or not? It is questions like these that exploit whatever insecurity there is within an individual and stimulate destructive emotions which he in turn carries with him into his home and into his church. In the case of young people this occupational situation is, of course, their school life with its adjustment to teachers, fellow students, curricular and extracurricular activities.

We can see therefore that one is not only unable to understand himself apart from the dynamic relationships of his past and present but that any adequate understanding of his problem must include also a knowledge of the particular socio-economic and religious group to which he belongs together with the general spirit of the times.

Since it is evident that people's problems have their ramifications as well as their origins in these significant areas in their life, it is also evident that the counseling that comes to grips with these problems must touch upon these areas. The pastor needs to remind himself as he attempts to meet this need for understanding that he is not primarily to get things clear in his own mind but in his counselee's mind. Otherwise the interview may, as with the taciturn individual, degenerate into a question-and-answer type of diagnosis. It is easy in this heyday of psychology for the pastoral counselor to think of himself as much an amateur psychologist as a pastor. His appetite for analyzing needs analyzing itself. It may be a disguised form of pride; if one can analyze another he is in a sense his superior. It may also be a manifestation of his impatience: let's put two and two together and get this thing over with. It may even be an outlet for his own anxiety: if he can understand the problem as he goes along he feels more secure in his role as the counselor.

The role of the counselor is not simply to get the information concerning the dynamic relationships in the life of the counselee but to stimulate him to *express* himself in these significant areas. It is possible for the counselor to have too much previous data on the counselee. Because he already knows this or that about him he may lose sight of the more important need that the counselee give expression to this information himself. Also he may allow this information to give direction to the counseling process which only the dynamic of the interview itself should give. When we know this or that about an individual we have the tendency to twist what he says or does not say to fit our explanation based on our previous knowledge.

How can the counselor get into these deeper levels of the problem? If he tries the third-degree process or any similar method of probing he more than likely will stir up resistance and the counselee may clam up in the very area the pastor is trying to open up. Our task is not merely to encourage the counselee to relate the nature of these relationships. In the first place such a procedure could very easily by-pass the release of the destructive emotions connected with these relationships. We get the picture but not the therapy. In short we try to satisfy the need for understanding without satisfying the need for confession, while actually the understanding should grow out of this release of feelings. In the second place there is the danger that if the pastor makes it a deliberate policy to dig out the childhood roots of each problem, he will only give his counselee something to account for his problem. If he has any inclination toward inertia he may use such information to excuse himself for his present inadequacies and to blame his parents. Understanding is the prelude to overcoming when it is the product of the counselee's own insights which he receives in his relationship to his counselor in the course of giving expression to the negative feelings generated in the critical areas of his past and present. The theological word for insight of this nature is wisdom. We find in the Old and New Testaments considerable emphasis on the desirability of achieving this wisdom. The records of the sages in both Testaments show that their wisdom was attained through a frank and open relationship with God in which they gave an honest expression of their feelings.

If certain of these relationships are close to his problem the counselee will probably allude to them during the counseling process. If the counselor is alert to the importance of these relationships he will respond to this allusion so that the counselee will continue to talk about it. The counselor needs patience to wait for the counselee to take the initiative to enter into these significant areas; he may also want to give a few stimuli to encourage this initiative. Even a question, if it is sufficiently casual, may be in order. "How does your wife (husband, mother, father, girl friend) feel about your problem?" may be the incentive needed to enter a vital area for understanding. Whatever the stimulus, it must be subtly handled so that it does not backfire and slow up the process. Normally it is better to take the road that is safe than to take the short cut that is hazardous. If the counselor has established a large amount of rapport with his counselee he can take more short cuts. On the other hand it takes time to develop this kind of rapport.

Bob was having a problem over whether he should study for the ministry. While at a religious camp the problem became acute and he discussed it with the camp counselor.

Bob: I've been wondering if I should study for the ministry. I've been thinking about it for some time now.

Counselor: I see. (A remarkably restrained response for a minister to such a statement. Usually the pastor's enthusiasm for gaining recruits overwhelms his good counseling sense in this area.)

Bob: It means going to college, and I don't know about that. I'm the only one on either side in my family even to finish high school.

Counselor: You feel that for you to attempt college with this background is a pretty big step.

Bob: I do. Beside I'll have to finance it myself. I don't know whether I can make it. (This indication of no family support raises a possible question in the counselor's mind concerning Bob's family relations.)

Counselor: You are wondering if you will be able to carry the load. (The counselor continues the straight listening approach that he has been following, even though he desires to explore into the above cue.)

Bob: That's about it.

Counselor: And how do your folks feel about it, Bob? (The lack of any further contribution from Bob in his preceding response opened the door for this question. The counselor felt he would facilitate the progress of the interview by actively pursuing at this point the counselee's previous "allusion by omission." He also felt that in his particular relationship to Bob he would raise no resistance to this direction. The fact that circumstances sometimes make impossible succeeding interviews influences the pastor's decision to use a directing question. It should be noted that the counselor asked his question in as casual a manner as possible.)

BOB: They try to discourage me. They don't think I'll make it. You see, I have a stepfather. He and I don't get along too well.

COUNSELOR: Oh. (The counselor got more than he bargained for. His motive for the rather neutral "oh" was "do no harm.")

BOB: I think he is jealous of me. When mom tries to stick up for me he accuses us of ganging up on him. He has never even wanted me to call him dad.

COUNSELOR: He feels that you are in some way a rival of his with your mother. (The counselor, having opened up this vital area with his question, continues in the listening approach to encourage the full exploration of this area. So we see that his question was no disruption of the listening process but rather an extension of it.)

BOB: I honestly think he would like to have me out of the house. He's almost said so in so many words. It gives you the feeling you are not wanted—that you are in the way. If I went to college it might be better all the way around. Yet I don't think I could ever go back home.

THE DEVELOPMENT OF INSIGHT

The manner in which the need for understanding is satisfied in the counseling process is a fascinating experience. It is a thrill to both counselee and counselor when the counselee gains a fresh insight into his problem. His experience is similar to the mystic's reception of revelation, as unexpectedly the light dawns and a new awareness possesses his mind. Insofar as the mystic is engaging in a counseling relationship with God the comparison is even more significant. It is a growing and at times overwhelming process of realization that readily lends itself to a religious interpretation. Through these insights the counselee "sees" the rational explanation for his problem which in turn gives him a measure of security. To discover also that he is not unique in his problem—that others are bothered with the same thing—helps to decrease his anxiety.

Perhaps the most significant part of this achievement of insight is the counselee's realization of his own contribution to his problem. People with problems rarely achieve this insight when they keep their problems to themselves because theirs is usually a continuous attitude of defense, particularly as these problems are associated with their relationships with other people. Since intimate relationships of this nature are often of a coercive stripe, whatever realization one may have of his responsibility in these difficulties is pushed into his unconscious in self-defense. It is obvious therefore that coercion must be kept out of the counseling interview. When the counselee is aware that the counselor is different—that his approach is the opposite of coercion—he is encouraged to lower his guard. Through the stimulation of the listening approach the repressed awareness of personal responsibility may re-enter the consciousness. Since there is no threat on this occasion the counselee may accept this insight.

This does not mean however that he must. Although he may realize his responsibility he may not yet be ready to act upon it. As one individual said to his pastor after several counseling interviews: "I'm beginning to wonder if, before I can solve my problem, my personality has to change. Frankly I don't see where this is possible." He did not return for his next appointment. He may still come back. There is an element of sovereignty—no matter how small—in the human personality that is not only the basis for personal responsibility but also is the insurance that a person is not the automatic outcome of any environmental process—even pastoral counseling. This limitation of pastoral counseling is inherent in the nature of man as described by the *imago Dei.* God made man free like himself. This means that God limited himself in his dealings with man. His self-consistency demands that he respect the freedom which he gave when he created man, even though this means he must accept man's rejection of his overtures. Jesus had to watch the rich young ruler turn and walk away, even though it filled him with sorrow.

Another significant characteristic of this development of insight is the realization of ambivalent feelings in the problem. These conflicting powers usually have their origin in the dynamic relationships in the counselee's life. A person may both love and hate a member of his family, he may desire both to submit and to attack, and this conflict leaves him immobile, locked in a self-against-self struggle. These ambivalent feelings extend also toward oneself and toward the ventures of life. The common difficulty in making decisions illustrates this extension and projection of these basic ambivalent feelings.

Since he is not supposed to hate or to attack a loved one, an individual feels guilty over this ambivalence and in a defense against the resulting anxiety may repress the undesirable feelings. The counselor's role is to be alert for any expression of insight by the counselee into ambivalent feelings so that he may respond by restating this insight. In this manner he clarifies the ambivalence so that the counselee may continue to face what may be the basis of his problem and to come to grips with it.

A businessman with a record of failures came to his pastor for counseling. In the course of this relationship he gained insight into his own responsibility for these failures.

MR. BOWLES: Sometimes I wonder if I'm not afraid of success.

PASTOR: On the one hand you desire it and on the other you shy from it.

MR. BOWLES: Yes, as though I *shouldn't* have it.

PASTOR: You want to succeed but are not sure that you should succeed.

MR. BOWLES: Perhaps it's that I'm not sure I deserve it.

The interview continued on the basis of this insight into Mr. Bowles' feelings of unworthiness or guilt which bring about his own unconscious co-operation with failure.

At the close of an interview that has been productive of insights the pastor may summarize these gains as a means of consolidating them. In this manner he ties the loose ends into a coherent whole. It is important that in this summary he refers to the insights gained as those of the counselee. As a precautionary measure he may ask the counselee to check him as he goes along to be sure that he has understood what the counselee meant to communicate and that he neither adds nor leaves out anything. Care must be taken not to use the summary as a surreptitious means of *giving* insights to the counselee. Beside being unethical the counselee may recognize these additions as not his own even in their cryptic form and resist rather than accept them.

We return to Kenneth Baltus, a portion of whose first counseling interview was recorded in chapter one. He is the "personality-conscious" young man who has been unable to feel accepted by people or to form any lasting relationships with the opposite sex, and suffers extreme moodiness because of it. During the counseling process he discovered insights into his personality structure and his home influences that enabled him to experience a measure of progress. However as often happens with deep-seated problems of long-standing he experienced a relapse. The following excerpt from the sixth interview is from this period of retrogression.

KENNETH: I wish I could get back to where I was. But I feel I can't. I've been so terribly moody, even when I expected the opposite. As hard as I try I'm still miserably unhappy.

PASTOR: It's hard to take a relapse after you were getting along so well.

KENNETH: It seems that everything concerned with my religion before was a shell. I really had a *front*. I didn't even recognize it myself. (He shows the insight gained in the preceding interviews and yet at present it depresses him.)

PASTOR: You feel that you were different on the outside than on the inside.

KENNETH: Yes, and what bothers me is that I don't feel guilty about it. Even in my prayers I catch myself defending myself to God.

PASTOR: Instead of feeling guilty you desire to justify yourself.

KENNETH: I catch myself talking to God like I talk to people. I try to smile and talk nice. But I seem to rate second class. In a crowd nobody directs their attention my way. Sometimes they get a little rough in the way they talk to me. I try to defend myself in a friendly way. I never get angry. I just keep smiling like I know I should. (In his relationship with people he shows little awareness of a facade.)

PASTOR: When they treat you shabbily you show no resentment toward them.

KENNETH: No. I try to please them like you should. I don't know what it's like to feel angry. Maybe it's that I don't feel, *period*. Like I was deadened inside.

While the pastor listened with his tongue in his cheek, he did not attempt to discount Mr. Baltus' insistence that he never knew anger. Inwardly however he felt that his counselee's deadness of feelings was due to his repression of the negative emotions rather than to their absence. Two interviews later showed a sudden turn in events.

KENNETH: I don't know what's the matter. I'm getting worse instead of better. I don't want to be around people any more, it seems.

PASTOR: How does it show itself, Ken?

KENNETH: Oh, like at social gatherings where I should be enjoying myself, I feel like chewing everybody's head off—and there's no reason for it.

PASTOR: An irritation comes over you.

KENNETH: Yes, I just get irritated all over—don't even care to talk.

PASTOR: Everybody makes you mad.

KENNETH: I hate myself for it—but I can't control it—I just don't care to be decent to people.

Here was the repressed anger coming out. Through the successive interviews of the counseling relationship layer after layer had been peeled off until the real problem was exposed. The long-buried anger was freed and gushed forth with such intensity that it was indiscriminate in its direction. This time the conscience censor could not keep it down. The conscious experience of anger was such a shock to Kenneth that it took him some time to figure it out. Then he realized that resentment had been a part of his life before and very much so, but that his feeling of guilt over it had caused him to repress it. Now that he was able to experience it again, he had his great opportunity to handle it honestly and courageously in the presence of God. The pastor's acceptance is the encouragement Kenneth needs to believe in the acceptance of God.

The pastor continued with the listening approach in the succeeding interviews and Kenneth continued to gain insight into his facade and to grow in the wholesome release of destructive emotions. After the termination of the interviews the pastor asked Kenneth to write up his insights for purposes of research. The portion included here, showing how the need for understanding was met through the counseling process, is with Mr. Baltus' permission.

". . . Another false understanding consisted of repressing feelings of anger, hate, disgust or disappointment. I often repressed feelings for other reasons but at this point I will refer only to my 'Christian' motive. I had the understanding that a Christian is a quiet, peaceful, humble individual who never raises his voice or gets angry, or becomes disturbed. It would be very much against the teachings of the Bible, I thought, ever to allow yourself to express anger, fear, hate, etc., and I was very sincere in this belief. According to this belief I tried to live my life. No wonder I stored up such anxiety and tension and nervousness. My ideas have changed now to the belief that a person should be himself at all times, and should try to rid himself of bad feelings (bursts of anger, disgust, etc.) through talking things over frankly with God.

". . . Probably one of the more important things I learned through my visits was to know how to let off emotions. I would repress many of my emotions, especially those of anger and hatred because I didn't want to hurt anyone, wanted to avoid useless arguments, or thought these emotions were unchristian. Now I have a greater understanding of what happens when these emotions are repressed, how they store up as potential explosives ready to burst out unsuspectingly in one form or another. Through your suggestion I began taking each situation for what it was worth and if I felt anger, I showed that anger. This was one of the finest and most helpful suggestions you could have given me—especially *me*. Since then I have experienced more peace and relaxation than I ever have before."

The suggestion to which he refers concerned our discussion at the close of the previously recorded interview over these new emotions. I suggested that he let these feelings out when they recurred rather than repress them. I did this because of his religious conviction that such was wrong, and my presence as a minister seemed to be retarding the natural maturation of conscience at this point. This takes us to the possible need for pastoral intervention in the counseling process.

WHEN INTERVENTION IS NEEDED

Perhaps we should say that there are exceptions to every rule or that no rule should overrule the spontaneity and ingenuity of personality, but there are times when the pastor's intervention may be needed. Students of harmony must learn adequately all the rules of the science and to use these rules with skill before they are allowed to set aside these rules for any indulgence in the dissonants of modern music. So the pastor should saturate himself in the listening approach before he allows himself to depart from it on occasion.

The pastor who counsels to any extent may think he recognizes the pattern of the problem before the counselee has fully expressed it. As we shall see more fully in the next chapter it is wise to hold back his analysis and to help the counselee to arrive at this understanding himself. The pastor's analysis is based on a backlog of experience which his counselee does not have. Therefore the counselee cannot be expected to see the wisdom of the pastor's interpretation as clearly as the pastor himself.

Until the counselee has grown in his own understanding of his problem, any analysis of it that his counselor may present is premature. Consequently he may reject his interpretation and as a result lose some of his confidence in him. Furthermore the counselee's ability to arrive at his own solution to his problem is dependent in part on his having achieved his own understanding of his problem. The counselor's analysis therefore is in danger of usurping the responsibility of the counselee and hindering his progress toward maturity.

There are times however when an individual gets hung up on a snag and seems unable to free himself. Often his difficulty lies in a conscience that is tyrannized by guilt and fear. This conscience usually has the sanction of religion and even the thought of breaking its hold is rejected as blasphemous. The presence of the pastor as the representative of religion is an even further deterrent to any thought of emancipation. When in the course of the counseling process all progress seems to be stymied because of this obstacle the counselor may have to intervene and attempt to clear the way.

Before he decides to make his intervention the pastor should be sure that he has allowed the counselee every opportunity to remove the block himself. Such intervention can be compared to surgery, to which the physician resorts only after less drastic means have been exhausted. Above all it is important that he have built up rapport sufficient to support his intervention. If an individual has confidence in his pastor he interprets a direct approach of this nature as frankness rather than coercion. So long as it is used with discretion it need not create any feelings of dependence upon the counselor. We shall reserve our example of this intervention for the next chapter, since it is often because of the counselee's subconscious refusal to assume responsibility that this intervention is needed.

INDOCTRINATION AND THE NEED FOR UNDERSTANDING

There is confusion over the relationship between counseling and indoctrination. To some, indoctrination has an odious ring and has no place in the counseling relationship. To others, indoctrination is the answer to the counselee's need for understanding. If those in the former group who react negatively to the word indoctrination will identify it temporarily with religious education, we will be able to discuss the subject with a common understanding of our terms. In indoctrination the pastor communicates religious truth to the counselee. This procedure has usually failed in the counseling relationship because the counselee is often too blocked emotionally either to receive or to comprehend the doctrines. It is of little value to exhort people to repeat doctrinal formulae, regardless of how true they may be, if they are not straightened out inside enough to carry through on these proposals. The familiar appeal to will power or even to conscience in behalf of this or that Christian doctrine can only further frustrate those whose personalities are already locked in emotional conflict.

Counseling as we have been describing it is a means of removing the block that prevents doctrine from taking hold. In this process the counselee gains insight into the truth about himself and the nature of life. If the pastor responds to these insights by dovetailing them with the related Christian doctrine he is indoctrinating in the most effective manner. Fortified by their association to an article of faith the counselee's insights may become even more meaningful to him. There are times also when the pastor may stimulate the counselee to these insights by his communication of a significant doctrine.

The attribute of the image of God by which man internalizes knowledge to become an individual is his reason. Destructive emotions resulting from his rebellion against God have disturbed his reasoning ability so that he is unable to understand how God is triumphant over evil. Releasing these destructive emotions through self-expression enables the mind to comprehend the gospel. The counselee can *see* that the serpent's head is crushed, and the way is open for him to enter into the covenant with God that brings security in a world of evil. In the language of the theology of the church the Holy Spirit works through a personal ministry to reveal the Word of God to the counselee.

SUMMARY

A large portion of a person's problem is usually below the surface of his understanding. When he faces a mystery he feels helpless to cope with it. Before he can solve his problem he has to get it out into the open where he can take a look at it. When he sees how everything works together and has its own rational explanation he is able to handle his problem more intelligently and confidently. The biggest enigma of all is oneself. People with problems are usually confused over the origin of their feelings or the nature of their motives. To make things more complicated they may not want to know the truth. The story behind the problem may not be pleasant and the counselee may just as soon run away from it as face it. He learns to rationalize and to scapegoat and succeeds not only in deceiving others but also himself.

Here is where the presence of the counselor is needed. He encourages the counselee to objectify his problem by talking about it. During the process of counseling he may give expression to things he had not realized before. Since these insights originate within himself he is not inclined to reject them. In an atmosphere devoid of coercion, the unpleasant truths about himself that he heretofore had repressed may re-enter his consciousness and this time be accepted.

CHAPTER FIVE

The Need for Growth

The understanding that a person receives in the course of the counseling process could perhaps have been given to him by the counselor during the first interview. At that time however it probably would have had little meaning to him. Something in the meantime has changed within him so that he can see the value in this understanding. This change is his degree of growth. Through the release of his destructive emotions and his relationship with the counselor he grows to the point where he arrives at this understanding himself. Even if the counselor had indicated this understanding before, the counselee may be unable to recall this fact, as he is overwhelmed by the newness of these insights as his own. Growth therefore is both a prerequisite to the satisfaction of the need for understanding and a result of this satisfaction.

RESPECT FOR PERSONALITY

The emphasis in counseling goes beyond the problem and centers in the person. The personality pattern of the counselee has its bearing on his problem and may be a problem in itself. To solve only the problem of the moment may leave the counselee inadequate to meet the next problem that comes his way. This would be a short-sighted goal because the counselee would be dependent upon the counselor for each new problem. A goal more worthy of the name would include the growth and maturity of the counselee. Therefore it follows that the pastor should not solve the problems of his counselees but help them to learn to solve them themselves.

The philosophic structure of counseling rests upon the prerogative of the individual to make his own decisions regarding choices that affect his life. Since his problem is obviously his own, the counselor allows him to retain the responsibility for solving it. In the traditional interpretation of pastoral counseling the responsibility for the problem is transferred to the pastor and he in turn decides what should be done. In reality this transference is an escape from freedom into paternalism; it is contrary to the philosophy of a democratic society; it is contrary also to the theological concept of the universal priesthood which insists upon a free and equal access to the mind of God for every believer.

Contrary to its apparent efficiency this transference of responsibility from the counselee to the pastor actually hinders the solution of the problem. Problems with any depth are so closely associated with the ego of the counselee that it is a question whether they really can be solved by another. It is also possible that the paternalistic counselor may not even unearth these deeper problems. If he allows the transference of responsibility to take place when the counselee presents his initial problem he is in danger of fixing the counseling at this superficial level.

So long as the counselee feels the pastor will solve his problem he is not encouraged to help himself. The fact that another is taking the responsibility for the solution to his problem opens the door for a convenient escape should the counseling fail; he can blame the counselor. The fear of failure is a strong enough influence already in most people's lives without the counselor tempting them with such an easy way out of the obligation to try.

While it is true that the pastor may see the solution to the problem rather quickly it is also true that the counselee is capable of achieving this insight too. It is not the counselor's task simply to tell his counselee what he thinks is the solution. Counseling is no lecture job: the counselee is frequently the victim of one too many lectures as it is. Although we may hear something with our ears it may not register in our minds until it corresponds to something with which we have had experience. If the pastor will hold himself back until he has led his counselee to see the issues for himself, he will find that what his counselee has discovered for himself "takes" much better than what he may discover *for* him. The counseling process itself becomes the stimulus for the growth that is needed for this comprehension.

THERAPY THROUGH RELATIONSHIP

As counselor and counselee spend time together a relationship develops between them that has a healing power all in itself. The "good feeling" the counselee gets after he has unburdened himself to his counselor causes him to look forward to his interviews. Part of his problem may be his need for attention and appreciation. The pastor satisfies some of this need as the counselee and his problem become the center of attention during the interview. In addition this positive relationship of acceptance and affection is an antidote to the harmful influences arising out of the negative relationships in his life. The destructive emotions that develop out of these past relationships, and may be the basis of his problem, are gradually replaced by their constructive counterparts arising out of this new relationship. This is a practical demonstration of how the Holy Spirit works through a personal ministry to produce his *fruit*—love, joy, peace, etc.—in the sanctification process.

Counseling relationships that develop over several interviews may become warm relationships. Very often people with problems are lacking in any such relationship. Of those who have come to me with serious emotional maladjustments few if any have had a healthy relationship with their parents. Lacking this relationship in the home they are handicapped in forming friendships outside of the home. They are alone in the midst of people. Unattached and unbelonging they feel insecure and uninspired. Even as love and affection give security to personality, so the warm relationship with the pastor may be the dynamic for confidence to the counselee. He can feel that someone cares and so he must be of some value and importance. The pastor's acceptance of him encourages him to accept himself.

A close relationship is a relationship of love.[1] It is a social function and those who share in it are a part of something over and above themselves. This relationship with the pastor temporarily penetrates the pattern of self-centeredness that often characterizes people with problems. It is also the means for the rapport the pastor needs to be an effective influence in the life of his counselee. In the process of psychoanalysis there comes the time when the client "falls in love" with the analyst. This emotional dependence is helpful to the client during the crucial period of his analysis. Before the client may completely recover, the analyst must succeed in transferring this attachment to something outside of the relationship. Otherwise the client would continue to be dependent upon the analyst.

[1] For a thorough analysis of love, cf. Paul E. Johnson, *Christian Love*, (Nashville: Abingdon, 1950), and Ashley Montague, (ed.), *The Meaning of Love* (New York: Julian, 1953).

Some such procedure may also take place in the counseling relationship. While the counselee should not be dependent upon the counselor, he is dependent upon the counseling relationship. If the responsibility for the problem is kept with the counselee his process of growth will in itself resolve this transference. Since the relationship with the pastor is ongoing and not confined to the counseling process, whatever transference is needed may go from a counseling relationship to a co-operative relationship in the work of the church. The social security available within the beloved community, the *ekklesia*, is illustrated in the bond of union that is celebrated in the common participation at the Lord's Table in the Sacrament. The pastor also should lead his counselee to the most beneficial transference of all: a relationship with a man of God should be introductory to a relationship with God himself. According to the doctrine of the ministry the pastor is not simply a counselor but a minister of God and his task is not completed until he has effected this transfer from himself to God.

There is a time when the counselor may give verbal encouragement to his counselee. This is not what is commonly known as giving reassurance. When the counselor is generous with his comment that everything is going to be all right or that things may not be as bad as they seem, he may only succeed in keeping the problem suppressed and in convincing his counselee that he does not understand. The generous use of the compliment can be a camouflage of this silver-lining approach and usually has the same effect. The counselee however is concerned about what other people think of him. Since his problem often centers in his feelings of inferiority he may imagine the worst if he is in doubt about their opinion of him. Naturally he wonders also what his pastor thinks of him. If occasionally the pastor will say a word or two—perhaps at the conclusion of the interview—to let him know that he has confidence in him, it will give him the encouragement and inspiration that he needs. It will relieve some of the anxiety that comes from wondering and not knowing. It is one of those honest expressions of friendship that do so much to establish this therapeutic relationship.

OUR AXES TO GRIND

Many of the problems that people bring to their pastor are the kind in which the counselee is at a loss to make a decision. While the pastor may agree theoretically that his purpose is to help the counselee make his own decision and not to make it for him, he usually has his own ideas on what decision he would like to see made. Even though he has no intention of influencing his counselee he still may have difficulty avoiding it.

Mrs. Bonham was going through the adjustment period following her divorce from her husband. During my counseling with her it seemed quite evident that her ex-husband was about as incapable of married life as one could imagine. He was guilty of adultery, cruelty, and non-support. Although he continued to coax her to return to him, she had no assurance that he would be any different than before. Yet it was not easy to live with her parents and care for and support her children. In spite of these difficulties she still felt that she should not return to him. I held the same opinion but I tried to be careful to keep my opinions out of our interviews.

We did not have any regular appointments and after a couple of weeks had passed without any word from her I began to wonder how she was getting along. The next Sunday at church I inquired for her. Her mother told me that she had gone back to her husband. Naturally this took me by surprise. I was puzzled that she did not tell me. Her mother also could not understand why she had not called me. Later when I saw her she apologized. "I knew I went against your advice and I was ashamed to tell you," she said.

It so happened that the remarriage did not work out, but that is beside the point right here. Mrs. Bonham said I advised her not to go back to her husband and I am sure I said no such thing. Either I exposed my feelings through the more subtle ways of voice inflection, facial reaction, or ominous silence which a sensitive person can pick up, or she simply ascribed to me the accepted opinion of her parents and friends. But because she felt I was on one side of the fence, she would not come to me when she decided to go to the other side.

It is a temptation for a pastor to project his own ideas into the counseling process and to try to arrange things as he would like to see them. He may do it unconsciously. When his young people bring to him their courtship problems, for example, he may be more of a Dan Cupid than a counselor. Like a lot of other people, he has his opinions concerning who should marry whom. He may also wonder what such a fine girl as Mary can see in a smart-aleck like Joe. When he counsels with Mary he may show his bias. He could be right in his opinion: on the other hand he could be wrong. If he reminds himself of this and of the damage his bias can do to his counseling relationship with Mary, he is taking the precautions necessary to safeguard his role as a counselor from the threat of his own interference.

The pastor is a preacher as well as a counselor. These two functions of his ministry can be a powerful team in helping people with problems. Their close association also has its complications. The pastor may suspect that those whom he is trying to help through counseling would co-operate with him and attend church. But they don't always do it. And it is often those whom he feels would profit most from his sermon who do not show up. He may find that his patience wears a little thin with these individuals. Also when they absent themselves often they are in danger of offending his ego. A pastor and his sermon are closely identified: if one has no use for the pastor he will probably not gain much from the sermon; and if the counselee shows little concern about coming to church, the pastor may find it hard to feel the same toward him as toward the appreciative. Any negative feelings that the counselor has toward the counselee will interfere with his understanding of him. They also may cause him to grow impatient with the growth process in favor of a few pointed directives. Because he has thrown his own negative emotions into the situation, this approach may lead to conflict between himself and his counselee.

These many influences within the pastor that predispose him to encroach upon the right of the counselee to solve his own problem reveal how important it is for him to understand himself. So long as he himself is insecure he will tend more to sabotage than to encourage the growth process. It takes a man who has achieved a measure of freedom himself to encourage others toward this same freedom.

THOSE WHO AVOID RESPONSIBILITY

The pastor may at times also receive a great deal of encouragement (or temptation) from the counselee to assume the responsibility for the problem. It is characteristic of certain individuals to avoid any personal obligation to mature. Some have devious ways of trapping the pastor into taking over this responsibility even against his better intentions. They may come with a question, often abstract and intellectual, get the pastor to commit himself, and then fix the counseling at this level by cross-examining his answers or even arguing against them.

These individuals are not ready to face their real problems, let alone take the responsibility for doing anything about solving them. The object of the counselor is to use the counseling process to stimulate their growth to where they will be ready for both. Yet this may be no easy task. These individuals may resist our intentions even to the point of sabotaging the listening approach by backing away from our restatements of what they themselves have said.

This type of a counselee often has a need for his problem. In his ambivalence over solving it he may resist anything positive in the interview—particularly the pastor's attempts, either direct or indirect, to point out or emphasize the encouraging side of things. They want help—yes—but not at the level where their problem lies. To the counselor they seem to say something like this: "I need help and I hope you can give it to me. Yet I doubt if you can, and I am going to see if I can't prove I'm right."

Burton Swan was such a counselee. He was a well-educated man in his late twenties. The following excerpts from his counseling interviews will illustrate this resistance to the growth process.

BURTON: Dr. Brooks said I should see you. I haven't been feeling well and he's been trying to fix me up, but I guess he thinks there's something bothering me. (He places both the responsibility and purpose for his coming upon his physician.)

PASTOR: Do you feel he is right? (He tries to get Burton at least to acknowledge that he has a problem.)

BURTON: Well—yes. As I told him I have no faith in anything. I get so low at times I wonder what's the use of going on. I think if I had a faith, things would be different. But it has to be a faith I can accept.

PASTOR: You feel the need for a faith, but it has to be a faith you can honestly believe in. (The pastor tries to capture the thought of what Burton has expressed.)

BURTON: Isn't that the way it should be?

PASTOR: Why, yes, I believe our faith should be intellectually respectable, if that is what you mean. (He is taken off guard by Burton's question concerning his restatement.)

BURTON: But how are you supposed to get it? (He has the pastor on the defensive.)

PASTOR: Well, let's take a look at it. Suppose you tell me what all you have done in regard to it. (A desperate attempt to get the counselee back in the center of the stage.)

BURTON: Oh, I go to church, of course, but I don't get anything out of it. I find myself questioning everything—seeing all the holes in it.

PASTOR: You dispute it before you accept it.

BURTON: Well, shouldn't I? I've got to have a faith I can accept. Yet I can't accept what the church teaches. That's my trouble.

PASTOR: It seems contrary to your reason, is that it? (His previous experience with Burton's questioning approach enables him to take this challenging statement in his stride.)

BURTON: I wouldn't say that. I don't know whether I believe or not. I think if I were with an atheist I'd argue for belief. That's just it—how do you know when you believe? (Burton is sensitive to the tendency of the listening approach to place him in the "driver's seat," and he fights it.)

PASTOR: You find yourself rebelling against anybody who acts as though he were sure. (The pastor has profited from past experience and refuses to swallow the question-and-answer bait.)

BURTON: Yeah. It irritates me if somebody tries to tell me—this is it! I can't take anything from anybody I feel is inferior to me intellectually. That's why I came to you. I think if you told me, I'd accept it.

This was too much for the pastor and he introduced Burton to the clever reasoning he had been holding in the back of his mind concerning the inevitability of faith—how that to disbelieve in God was also a faith. Thus Burton's problem, he pointed out, was not a question of faith or no faith, but of *which* faith. After several apparently interested queries Burton said, "Sure I can see that. But it doesn't help me to believe."

The pastor is now faced with a defense of his position which he could "win" only by superior logic. The "counseling" would then have probably continued around an intellectual debate on the nature of faith. He could also gracefully retreat. Fortunately he chose the latter. Before long Burton was back again on the subject of his questioning frame of mind.

BURTON: I've been told what to believe when I was a kid. Now I keep questioning whether I believe or not.

PASTOR: You find yourself arguing with what you were told in the past. (Grateful that he has been given another chance, the pastor is careful not to muff it.)

BURTON: I'll admit I'm argumentative. Maybe it's because I feel frustrated or something—I don't know.

PASTOR: You don't feel you are getting along as well as you would like?

BURTON: No—I get awfully disgusted—I suppose with myself. (etc.)

The interviews continued in a more or less erratic manner in the direction indicated by Burton in the above conversation, in which he began to acknowledge his real problem. Although people like Burton seem to defy the listening approach, they will usually succumb to it if the pastor is able to resist all the pressures to abandon it. And since this approach keeps the seat of the responsibility with the counselee, it should ultimately stimulate his growth. Of course there is no automatic guarantee that it will. But if it does not, the pastor can rest assured that he would have met with failure also had he given in to the argumentative design of his counselee. In the latter, however, his chances for making things worse are much greater.

There are also those who come to the pastor and expect him to solve their problem. Their persistent avoidance of responsibility stymies the whole process. As an example of this attitude Mr. Thornton was outstanding. The pastor was having a harried time keeping the initiative for the problem with the counselee. In describing various areas of his problem and background Mr. Thornton would continually ask, "Do you see any clue in this?" After avoiding the question several times the pastor thought it would be helpful to the interview to structure the relationship.

MR. THORNTON: ". . . Do you see any clue yet?"

PASTOR: That isn't really the issue, Mr. Thornton, because you are the only one that can really know.

MR. THORNTON: How do you mean?

PASTOR: As you talk things over with me, the purpose is to help you to discover what's behind your problem and also to decide what you want to do about it.

MR. THORNTON: I was afraid of that. In other words you mean it's up to me.

PASTOR: In a sense, yes. Let's put it this way: I'm here to help you to help yourself.

MR. THORNTON: I see. I guess I was hoping for an easy answer. But I don't suppose there is any. Maybe that's my trouble. I'm looking for the easy way.

This illustrates a specific area for the occasional need for intervention described in the last chapter. Following the confession in the last statement the pastor responded to the feelings expressed, and the counseling process began to take on a sense of direction.

THOSE WHO ARE NOT READY TO GROW

Even as the sheer intensity of their pain is all that will drive some people to their physician, so the degree of psychic pain brings some individuals to their pastor. Since their pain is from the pressure of accumulated negative feelings, they satisfy their need for confession in talking to the pastor and find relief. Just as the pastor feels he has gotten the emotions to subside so that he can get down to business on the source of the problem, the counselee may announce at his next interview that all is well. The pastor feels of course that such is not the case—that while the infection is drained, the condition causing the infection remains. Yet this counselee may not care to go any further: relief from immediate pain is all he desires.

Since the pastor knows his negative feelings will probably accumulate again, he may try to continue counseling with him. If he handles things in a casual manner, he may succeed. Since the press is removed, however, this counselee may show little interest in discussing his problem any further, and may give the impression that the pastor is creating a problem. Though it bothers him to do so, the pastor may do well to accept the counselee's verdict in this matter. Such a person may need to suffer further before he can satisfy his need for growth. Because he has had to declare his problem solved, there is a danger that he will not return to the pastor when the trouble recurs. The pastor, therefore, should prepare him before he leaves so that he may return without feeling any loss of face.

SIGNS OF MATURITY

The goal of the counseling process is the growth of the counselee. If the counselor keeps the responsibility for the problem with the counselee he can normally expect to reach his goal. As the counseling relationship moves toward this goal he will begin to notice the signs of developing maturity. These are signs of a growing independence from the counselor. There is an ego-satisfaction in being needed: the counselor may have to remind himself to encourage these signs of growth.

Even as he retains the responsibility for his problem the counselee also makes the decision to discontinue the interviews. As long as he desires to meet with the counselor he probably does not feel strong enough to go on his own. When he does suggest that it may be unnecessary to continue his appointments the counselor can take this as the sign that he has outgrown his need for the interviews. Let him accept the verdict and trust that he has done a good job.

In the meantime he needs faith in the principles of counseling. When he counsels with those whose problems are deep-seated there will be those times when he does not seem to be getting anywhere. About the fifth to sixth interviews he may feel like abandoning these principles for a more drastic approach. These principles, however, will prove their worth if he persists in their use. It may help him fortify this faith if he realizes that these principles have a basis not only in psychology but also in theology. While they have been developed by modern specialists from the needs of the troubled personality, they can be developed from and expanded through basic doctrines of the theology of the church.

According to Christian theology, growth in personality results from the experience of a relationship of love with God. Although the Christian means for growth are means of grace there is no growth outside of man's responsibility. God operates in view of this responsibility. This characterizes the pastor's approach to his counselee, for he also stimulates growth by a relationship of love that encourages the counselee's responsibility.

St. Paul illustrates this co-operative relationship between love and responsibility by two apparently contradictory statements in his letter to the Galatians. First he says, "Bear ye one another's burdens." Then he turns right around and says, "Every man shall bear his own burden." Looking deeper we see that these two directives are needed to balance each other. On the one hand we are to bear one another's burdens, for this is the meaning of love. In a relationship of empathy we have compassion on the sorrows of our neighbor and share them as our own with God in prayer. On the other hand we do not help people when we take the burden from their shoulder and place it on our own. The human personality does not grow this way; for each must bear his own burden. In this manner he works out with fear and trembling the salvation that has been given him. Counseling that is helpful does not remove this challenge from the counselee, but helps him to meet it. Our references to counseling, therefore, refer to this listening approach, leading to catharsis, clearing the way for insight, and stimulating the process of growth.

SUMMARY

We turn our attention to a more penetrating analysis of the theological doctrines that support and expand these principles of counseling, with their application to the counseling process. Theology not only adds something to these psychological principles, but these principles themselves are oriented in the same theological frame of reference as the increment that enhances them. Rather than feeling constrained to solve his counselee's problem the counselor should help him to solve his own problem. The emphasis in the counseling process is not only on the problem, but on the person who has the problem; the goal is not only the solution of the problem but the maturation of the counselee, that he may better handle his future problems. The personality of the counselee is often the basis of the problem or may even *be* the problem.

Although the pastor may see the solution long before the counselee, he is wise if he leads his counselee to the point where he can see the solution for himself rather than to tell him the answer before he is able to receive it. Many a fine solution to a problem has been rejected by a counselee simply because it was sprung on him before he had grown enough to see its wisdom. Once he has rejected it he may feel obligated to defend his rejection, thereby complicating even further the growth of his ability to understand.

CHAPTER SIX

The Concept of Man

Theology and psychology are both oriented in human experience. The tendency of doctrine to date itself to its age of formulation is more a problem of terminology than of intrinsic value. Its danger of becoming removed from life in its accumulation of age is more the fault of the dogmatician than of its content. The four needs of the troubled personality are anticipated in the teachings of the theology of the church. Because these doctrines contain the fundamentals of the clinical approach to the problems of the psyche, they form a theological basis for the principles of counseling.

The Christian concept of man is more or less fundamental to this theological correlation, as it deals with the nature and interpretation of the conflict in human personality that gives rise to the destructive emotions. This conflict is identified by the doctrine as the conflict between the way a man is and the way he was meant to be—between the image of God in which God created him and the corruption of that image in sin.

Regardless of what particular confession we consult the doctrine of man has these two parts: man as God created him, and man as he has become; the image of God, and the corruption of this image. In article VII of the articles of religion in the Methodist Discipline, for instance, we read:

> Original sin standeth not in the following of Adam (as the Pelagians do vainly talk), but it is the corruption of the nature of every man, that naturally is engendered of the offspring of Adam, whereby man is very far gone from original righteousness, and of his own nature inclined to evil, and that continually.

In Article III of the New Hampshire Confession we have this same teaching in a more modern terminology.

> We believe that Scriptures teach that Man was created in holiness, under the law of his Maker; but by voluntary transgression fell from that holy and happy state; in consequence of which all mankind are now sinners, not by constraint but choice; being by nature utterly void of that holiness required by the law of God, positively inclined to evil; and therefore under just condemnation to eternal ruin, without defense or excuse.

The original source material for this doctrine is the story of Adam and Eve in the Garden of Eden. To get a clear understanding of what the confessions mean to convey in this concept we turn to the opening chapters of the book of Genesis.

THE IMAGE OF GOD

This doctrine, along with the others in the theology of the church, has its origin in the Scriptures. Its original source material is the story of the creation and fall of man in the Garden of Eden. These opening chapters of Genesis portray the origin and nature of this conflict within. Here we read of the decision of the Creator to make man in his own image. To Adam and the helper he created for him, God gave the charge to be fruitful and multiply, to replenish and subdue the earth, to have dominion over the fish of the sea, the fowl of the air, and the animals on land, and to dress and keep the garden in which they were to live. They were free to eat of the fruit of all the trees of the garden with one exception: the tree of the knowledge of good and evil. Summing up the creation story the account states: "And God saw everything that he had made, and behold, it was very good."

It has been charged that instead of God creating man in his image, man has created God in man's image. The fallacy in this charge is more on *create* than on *man's image*. The meaning of the *imago Dei* is closely allied with the theological concept of the incarnation. Christ as the *Second Adam* is the representative (son of) man. He also is God in man (Son of God). Through his humanity he reveals divinity. In him we behold man to understand God and in perceiving God we understand man.

The first Adam is not an incarnation but a creation. His being is fashioned in the similitude of God but he is not God. He is the creature and not the Creator. The image of God is traditionally associated with those qualities of man that identify him as a self, a person, that differentiate him from the rest of creation. He is able to think abstractly and to be conscious of himself. His sensual perception is enhanced with aesthetic appreciation. He is a moral being, capable of moral knowledge, with freedom to make moral choices and with a sense of moral obligation. As God is love, so man is able to love, particularly his Creator, and his inner security is associated with this fellowship. Lastly we come to the quality of "original righteousness" or rather sinlessness.

One almost hesitates to mention this phase of the doctrine of man because it runs counter to current opinions of what is intellectually respectable.[1] Yet what is intellectually respectable in one age may be considered outmoded in the next. Consequently it may be more intellectually respectable to question what is generally accepted as intellectually respect-

[1] Cf. David Roberts, *Psychotherapy and the Christian View of Man* (New York: Scribners, 1951), pp. 86-93.

able rather than simply to accept it because it is generally accepted.

Churchmen who object to original righteousness feel it is untenable on the basis of the natural sciences. It cannot be denied that there are difficulties of adjustment in this area. The social factors in the current mood can also not be overlooked. Scholarship within the church is influenced by the emotional feud over evolution in the past generation. Churchmen have become embarrassed over these ecclesiastical conflicts with science and scientific theories and in most instances rightly so. In attempting to rectify the past they at times give the impression of leaning over backward. What was once a danger of antiscience within the church has become the danger of scientism. This is particularly true regarding the doctrine of man. Too often it seems that the thirst for the approval of the intelligentsia has led churchmen to the unscientific assumption that the present stage of science is supreme, even against their own Bible evidence.[2] A more objective approach would weigh each on its own merits, especially since the theories of evolution within the natural sciences have themselves been undergoing continuous realignment to the discoveries of new and sometimes disturbing evidence.

Perhaps part of the difficulty is also a misconception of the nature of original righteousness. It simply means that the division within man is not part of the Creator's design but is the result of man's decision to go against this design. There is nothing unhuman about a personality without this characteristic inner conflict. We see far more of this original righteousness in the *Second Adam* than is ever attributed to the first Adam. Yet as Jesus developed this righteousness within the realm of human experience, he in no way placed himself

[2] Cf. Fritz Kunkel, *In Search of Maturity* (New York: Scribners, 1943) Chapter 3 and specifically p. 21.

outside the human picture. Righteousness is a dynamic condition of mind that continues to create itself in each new experience in the human situation. The first Adam failed to meet this creative challenge in the development of his righteousness and lost the unity of personality inherent in the Creator's design. This experience of lostness continues to influence man's approach to his division within.

Original righteousness was not a quality indigenous to human nature as were the other qualities of the divine image. Its dynamic quality is in contrast to characteristics such as the capacity for moral knowledge and moral freedom which are of the substance of human nature. Original righteousness was sustained by the relation of fellowship between the creature and the Creator. The creature manifested this element of the image only because he was in position as a mirror to reflect the original in God before him. When this communion was disrupted through sin, original righteousness was lost. In a similar manner the return to this righteousness is by way of the restoration of this fellowship, as we shall see in the chapter on sanctification.

Although there are difficulties in adjusting this concept of original righteousness to certain theories of evolutionary development, we bring upon ourselves other difficulties from a counseling point of view if we abandon it. Original righteousness sets the stage for the explanation of sin (the doctrine of original sin), and when it is abandoned, the understanding of sin is also undermined. The resultant attempts to account for the ubiquity of sin as well as the nature of sin itself are, on the whole, inadequate so far as human experience is concerned, and, therefore, so far as the principles of counseling are concerned. There is a parallel between this ubiquity of sin and the widespread presence of personal problems, and this *in-common* relationship will have its effect on one's interpretation of these problems.

The explanation most clearly related to the evolutionary process defines sin as a lack of adjustment to the comparatively recent emergence of the human mind. The concentration camps of Buchenwald and Dachau reveal more of a perversion than a lack of adjustment. Sin at its worst is not animal-like, but devilish; not physical, but spiritual. Another theory attributes sin to ignorance. Education or knowledge, therefore, is the solution. This theory has nearly exhausted itself. Simply because a man understands what is right is no guarantee that he will do it. Knowledge need not affect the will. It was this fallacy that bankrupted the traditional concept of counseling and made mandatory the emergence of the new approach.

Others attribute sin to the evils of society. The sinner is more or less the victim of his environment. While the influence of the social situation is tremendous, one cannot escape individual responsibility because of it. The individual is the unit of society; he brings its evils into being and perpetuates them. Others realizing the shallowness of these interpretations have consigned the origin and explanation of sin to enigma.[3]

An inadequate interpretation of sin leads to an inadequate interpretation of human problems, and, in turn, to an inadequate therapy for the healing of the division within. All of these explanations in one way or another minimize man's responsibility for his sin or minimize sin by dissociating it from its judgment unto condemnation. The principles of counseling are derived from a *science* of sin—the clinical study of the guilty. We have learned that if we are to help these people, we must deal with them where they are. This means that any attempt on the part of the counselor to minimize sin,

[3] David Roberts, *op. cit.*, p. 107.

even with those whose sensitivity to their guilt is most acute, will slow up if not block the therapeutic process.

The principles of counseling as a science have no conflict with the historical interpretation of the doctrine of man. Since they are dependent upon encouraging resources already at work within the individual to cope with the division, they may even be said to corroborate it. The contrast between what a man is and what he was meant to be is intensified if this contrast were actually lived out in the human drama. According to the Jungian concept of the collective unconscious this experience would then be a part of the racial memory at work in archetypical symbols in the unconscious mind. This subconscious sense of *lostness* would be a *pull back* which would intensify the individual's desire to become righteous (heal the division), and hence would substantiate even further the validity of the principles of counseling.

ORIGINAL RIGHTEOUSNESS IN THE SECOND ADAM

Those who feel the origin of sin is an enigma cannot understand how one who was originally righteous could sin. What was wrong with him inwardly that he could choose to sin? Naturally a sin of the mind, or motives, preceded the external demonstration of the sin. The whole psychology of the temptation is directed toward motives. The Tempter first arouses the woman's curiosity over this knowledge (experience) of evil that she did not have. He hints that she is being taken advantage of by God; that if she partook of the fruit she would become as God. As she concurred in these thoughts she initiated a spirit of rebellion against her Creator, and became oblivious of all the other fruit in the garden to covet this one. After a series of rationalizations she carried through her rebellion by eating the fruit, and found in the man one who lacked only the initiative to take the same step.

Is there difficulty in conceiving how one who was perfect in his creation could be tempted to become covetous in spirit? Behind the corrupted motives is the moral freedom which is inherent in the person of God and in man created in his image. The very qualities that made man capable of righteousness also made him capable of unrighteousness. The temptation to sin was essentially a temptation to rebel against being a creature. The *Second Adam* had to undergo the same temptation. The purpose was the same—to stabilize his righteousness by exercising it. "Though he were a Son, yet learned he obedience by the things which he suffered."

In his forty days in the wilderness Jesus experienced in variant forms this temptation to rebel against his status. Each time he answered the Tempter in ways that structured his relationship to the Creator: "Man shall not live by bread alone, but by every word that proceedeth out of the mouth of God," to the temptation that he cease being "led by the Spirit"; "Thou shalt not tempt the Lord thy God," to the temptation that he use his power to glorify himself rather than the will of him who sent him; "Thou shalt worship the Lord thy God, and him only shalt thou serve," to the temptation that he rule as a Caesar-God. The incarnation in no way nullified his creatureliness in his role as the Second Adam. His victory in the Adamic temptation also shows that temptation itself, even though it is apparently internalized by mental recognition, is not corruptive. It is only when a personality participates in this temptation by decision (moral freedom) that he corrupts his motives. The result is also a corruption of this freedom—actually a slavery of soul in the direction of his choice to rebel. It is the purpose of the counseling process to release the counselee from this slavery. Pastoral counseling is particularly adapted to this purpose since it is backed by the Christian answer to this enslavement. When his freedom is "liberated" the counselee can progress toward the goal of maturity.

CORRUPTION IN SIN

We return again to the human drama in Genesis to illustrate the nature of this inner slavery. The experience of evil which man had gained through his rebellion against his creatureliness began immediately to create its repercussions within. Both the man and his wife felt an inner discomfort, a psychic pain. They became confused over what was happening to them. Theirs was the misery of a guilty conscience and in a desperate attempt to cope with it, they covered themselves with fig leaves. Although they had been naked before they did not become ashamed of it until after their rebellion. While not supporting the Freudian interpretation of human nature, this episode illustrates the affinity of sex for guilt. Not only is the guilt over sex often extremely severe, but guilt that originates elsewhere in an individual's life may readily spread to his sexual powers. Perhaps this is because the guilty person feels unworthy of the pleasure of sex and at the same time feels incapable of dispensing with its intense appeal. The result is an anxiety over this area of life.

Although they had covered their nakedness their pain continued. Adam and his wife became overwhelmed with fear and hid in the bush. Guilt destroys the security within a person. It creates a barrier in his relationship to God that makes him feel alone within and forsaken because of his sin. As a result he becomes anxious over what may happen to him and in desperation may try to run away.

Adam's reaction to guilt is typical of the individual who seeks to "solve" his problem by refusing to face it. His lack of success is also typical. Even in his hiding he hears the voice of God: "Adam, where art thou?" Like the guilty person that he is, Adam defends himself before he is really accused. "I was afraid, because I was naked; and I hid myself." He is not ready to face his real problem and so he adopts the familiar tactic of the escape artist: he rationalizes. The pain of guilt makes it tempting to give a better reason for our conduct than the real reason, and one may succeed in convincing not only others but himself that the better reason is the real reason.

But self-deception can never be thoroughly complete. The voice of God continues to batter away at its defenses. "Who told thee that thou wast naked? Hast thou eaten of the tree, whereof I commanded thee that thou shouldst not eat?" Adam is forced to face his sin. Yet he still is not ready to accept the responsibility for it; in fact he is resentful that his escape has failed. Like a trapped animal he attacks: "The woman whom thou gavest to be with me, she gave me of the tree and I did eat."

Blaming those whom we also love and respect for things for which we too are responsible is also contrary to the *imago Dei.* When the emotion of resentment subsides we feel guilty about this resentment. More guilt, however, leads to more anxiety which leads to more resentment. This is the slavery of sin of which Jesus spoke: "Everyone who commits sin is a slave to sin." Because these destructive emotions are not dispersed but rather intensified in this vicious cycle, they leave the individual in a frame of mind that predisposes him to sin again. This inward condition of separation from God that increasingly dissociates man from his original image is called death by the Scripture. "For in the day that thou eatest thereof thou shalt surely die." Like Freud's death instinct, this condition of separation is cumulatively self-destructive.

DOCTRINE OF SIN

The conflict between what a man is and what he was meant to be is based upon the qualitative difference between sin and righteousness. Man's decision to participate in the temptation to rebel introduced evil into his nature. The radical contrast between this new experience and the original righteousness in which he was created, produced a violent reaction—a clash-in-the-gears, as it were. This is evidenced by the release of the destructive emotions which not only perpetuate but increase this division. Becoming a part of his personality this division influences every activity of his personality—the ambiguity between sin and righteousness is characteristic of his being. Consequently the doctrine of man is not concerned with sins but sin. Individual sins are merely the peripheral manifestation of this inner corruption of the *imago Dei.*

The qualitative nature of this corruption of man's motives is illustrated also in the Eden account. The desire to be as God was coupled with the desire to know evil: the rebellion against the Creator was a rebellion also against the righteousness he represented. It was a denial of creatureliness that put him at enmity with the Creator and ultimately with his fellow creatures, because he had placed himself in a position of centrality that he could never occupy as a creature. The corruption in its essence is an egocentricity that isolates the self from other selves by a denial of love in the destructive emotion of resentment and hatred.

The predestination to egocentricity which the rebellion originated is described in the confessions as a "positive inclination to evil." Since this inclination is a part of him, the individual is helpless to rid himself of it—a slave of sin. Following the historic Augustinian stand on original sin the confessions find in the principles of counseling an ally against the Pelagian point of view. The idea that man is free to choose the good over the evil leads to a moralism that creates a legalistic flight into a righteousness of externalities. The danger is in the development of a facade behind which the individual "loses" consciousness of the morality of his motives. This unrecognized egocentricity of motive is the basis for many neurotic disorders.

When in addition to man's helplessness in his sin, the concept of original sin also asserts that man is responsible for his sin, it appears at best to be non-rational. The principles of counseling, however, rest on both of these conditions. It is because his inner conflict becomes too much for him that the counselee needs help. He is a slave of his destructive emotions. Yet except he retain the responsibility for his problem, he cannot be helped. Consequently the doctrine is not contrary to reason, if we consider reason to be based on experiential data.

The Adamic rebellion, according to the confessions, has become a part of human nature. The decision to rebel was so radical an innovation that it produced a radical change in the personality of the rebel. This corruption of the *imago Dei* was actually a change in the nature of personality—a mutation—which became a permanent characteristic of progeny in a reproduction "after its kind." From a confessional point of view "the last mutation" is an evolution in the mind of man in the direction of the diabolical. To say that the origin of sin is in man's own will does not contradict the doctrine that the individual from his beginning shares in the Adamic rebellion. The doctrine does not deny individual freedom but accounts for the fact that in the face of this freedom all seem to choose at various times to go Adam's way. To say that man sins because of his anxiety over his freedom, or because of social demands that provoke pride through comparison with others, or because of the obstacles he must transcend in becoming a self, all place sin outside the decision of the will; to say that man makes his own free decision to sin because of these internal and external influences only attempts to show

how the inheritance factor works, since all fall victim to these influences.

The nature of this inheritance of the corruption is no greater problem, genetically speaking, than the inheritance of personality itself. The difficulty is in accounting in terms of a physical science for the inheritance of the qualities of the human mind for which there is no physical explanation—whether they be the appreciation of beauty, the ability to think abstractly, or the capacity for moral freedom itself, of which original sin is simply a limitation. Actually the doctrine of original sin does not entail the contemporary concept of heredity, but simply maintains that since the fall of man the inclination to evil is part of the *given* in the potential for personality development.

In this whole picture of sin there is no attempt on the part of the doctrine of man to apologize for man because he is a person or to discourage his initiative to improve himself. Rather it attempts to describe the situation as it is—to give a realistic picture—not for the purpose of tearing man down, but to prepare the way for building him up. It must be admitted that the doctrine of sin has been abused. In attempting to defend it, some have treated it as an end in itself rather than a means to an end. Because they were defensive they seized upon each and every effect to support the cause, and hence distorted the spirit of a description of cause and effect that had as its purpose the elimination of the effect. The place of the doctrine in the theology of the church is not simply to describe man's helplessness but to lead him to his help. The theme throughout the doctrine is that man is redeemable. The concept of total depravity is often misunderstood. It does not mean that man has fully committed himself to evil for this would place him beyond redemption (as typified in the devil). Rather it means that there is nothing within man that can redeem him from his slavery to sin. Yet the very fact that he is called a slave implies that he may not be satisfied with his status. In the midst of his evil man is in conflict over it. And this conflict makes him redeemable.

The doctrine of man, therefore, presupposes a *gospel.* For man to be healed in his division within, he needs to have his relationship with his Creator restored. His harmony within will come from his harmony with his God. Since man is helpless in his slavery, his redemption is an act of the Creator. Pastoral counseling is a redemptive process by which a way is prepared for the reception of the gospel. In fact it is the gospel that supports pastoral counseling, since the principles of counseling are based on the reality of this acceptance.

The concept of man as sinner is balanced by the concept of man as a creation of God. Original righteousness is present in the sense of a potentiality. By holding in tension both original sin and original righteousness the doctrine of man presents a realistic picture of man as a child of God. In his fallen state man is an estranged child, but one with the potential for restoration. Creation and redemption are not divided concepts but must be viewed in a single glance. For this reason self-contempt is equal to self-exaltation in its violation of humility. Humility results from a realistic evaluation of the self, and those counselees who loathe themselves are in conflict with the evaluation of God. Man's growth is in the direction of reclaiming original righteousness, resulting in an increased limitation of original sin. This inherent self-worth in man, containing the possibility for divine redemption and growth, is fundamental to the philosophy of pastoral counseling.

DOCTRINAL BASIS FOR COUNSELING

The principles of counseling are oriented to a division within the personality of the counselee as described in the

Christian concept of man. They are a supportive stimulus to the *pull back* within the individual to heal this breach. This healing process is complicated by the defense mechanisms set up by the individual as supports for his ego in an egocentric structure of personality. By creating an acceptive atmosphere in the counseling relationship the principles of counseling encourage the pulling down of these defenses by making them unnecessary. In a relationship oriented to listening and understanding the counselee becomes increasingly aware that he is free to be himself and to express himself. So long as an individual feels "crowded" by the judgments of others upon him, he erects his defenses against these judgments, so much so that he is often unable to exercise his own judgment powers to any degree of objectivity. The realization that, so far as the external world is concerned, the "pressure is off" removes also the muffler from the voice of the judge within. The principles of counseling aim first at the elimination of self-deception in the counselee so that he may look at the basic cleavage within himself.

Akin to the spirit of the doctrine of man the principles of counseling are based on the necessity of facing the negative and of assuming one's responsibility for the negative. In the counseling procedure the radical nature of the contrast within is not to be minimized by the counselor. If he should attempt subtly to contradict the counselee by giving reassurance before the full scope of the division is accepted, he will hinder the solution to the problem, for he will meet with the defense of the guilt consciousness of the counselee and his attempts to console may only provoke the counselee to unconsolableness.

The principles of counseling along with the doctrine of man point up the fundamental position of guilt in the disturbances of personality. Since the sting of guilt is in the separation it produces between an individual and his God, the adequacy of any non-religious solution to this problem is doubtful. It would fail to meet the deeper level of anxiety that grows out of the break between man and his Creator, which can never be basically dispersed at the upper levels of human relationships.[4] In its emphasis on the dignity of God's creation, the doctrine maintains that fine but radical difference between hating sin and hating the sinner.

The counseling process reveals the way this conflict within the human personality described by the doctrine of man manifests itself in the problems of people. The corruption of pride, for example, can be responsible for severe guilt feelings. I have witnessed more self-contempt in guilt over pride among church people than in guilt over sex problems. This guilt usually occurs after some penetrating experience in which the individual is confronted with the self-centeredness of his motives which had heretofore eluded him. The realization is such a shock to him that he sees himself primarily in terms of his pride, losing sight of his inherent value as a human being, with the result that he rejects himself. Although the experience convinces him of the need for grace, he feels too despicable to receive it. As one counselee put it:

> I guess I'm just realizing what a hypocrite I am. My religion is a farce. It seems now that everything I've done has been motivated by pride. The worst of it is that others think of me as an exemplary Christian. In fact I did myself.

That humanity is "by nature sinful and unclean" seems to apply only to him; that there is divine forgiveness applies to everybody but him. He needs to see himself as still worth loving. Through the process of confession and a renewed understanding of the Christian gospel he achieved this insight.

[4] Cf. Fritz Kunkel, *op. cit.*, Chapters 4 and 5, specifically pp. 27-28 and 33.

Guilt of this nature is evidence of the individual's awareness of his own responsibility for his motives and of the pull within him to a righteousness that is complete.

Usually the conflict over pride is expressed more in terms of the frustration and dissatisfaction it creates concerning the individual's life as a whole. George Thomas was tense and uncomfortable around people, but when he withdrew his misery continued, for he was constantly berating himself for his failures in this and other areas. Progress was painfully slow at first in his counseling, but the following excerpt from a later interview shows a change.

THOMAS: I got a lot of criticism from my folks. I guess since then I sort of expect it from everybody. (When one is deprived of normal acceptance, his pride is stimulated defensively, creating within him an inordinate desire for that of which he has been deprived.)

PASTOR: You feel they will be critical of you because you have had plenty of criticisms in the past.

THOMAS: Could be. Anyhow I've always tried to be nice to people so they wouldn't be critical. But it doesn't seem to work either. (When we become agreeable to compensate for our feeling of inferiority, we lose our individuality and with it the interest and respect of others. Essentially this compensation shows a disrespect for the self.)

PASTOR: You don't feel any more accepted for being nice.

THOMAS: No, I don't seem to get any respect. Maybe it's my imagination too. I guess I think they can—well—see into me. (When one's motives for being nice are selfish, he is in fear this will be discovered.)

PASTOR: And do you feel that this would cause them not to respect you?

THOMAS: Well—yeah, I guess so, I've always felt I had to prove myself . . . . (pause)

PASTOR: As though by yourself, you couldn't stand inspection —unless you did something to gain some respect. (The pastor's response brings out the ever present need for atonement through achievement by those who feel guilty over themselves as persons.)

THOMAS: Right. That's me all over. If I just had some evidence that I was getting some place—but I don't.

PASTOR: That is you feel the need for something you don't have. Can you express what this is?

THOMAS: I don't know—it sounds sort of funny. I've always had the desire to be a leader—and, well, I seem to be anything but that . . . . (pause) (Feeling deprived in his early years of respect, his desire is for a compensating prestige.)

PASTOR: You have the desire to lead but you don't see any progress.

THOMAS: Well, not much. (pause) Maybe I think about it too much—I mean, without improving myself. But I'm always worried over how things are going to come out.

PASTOR: You have a hard time not thinking about these things when you are worried about them.

THOMAS: I keep wondering if there is still time. There is always something pushing me inside—as though I weren't going to make it. And I've got to be sure it's going to work out before I can stick at it. Kind of mixed up, isn't it? (The ego is fearful of being too late. It goads us forward and at the same time throws up a roadblock before us.)

PASTOR: You feel driven to accomplish your ambitions, but need to have the evidence that you will succeed in order to keep trying. (The pastor's response captures the expressed fact that pride cannot trust—it "walks by sight.")

THOMAS: Yeah. I suppose that's why I keep going from one thing to another. But this has to stop. I can't be doing this all my life, that's for sure. (The whole story of his ego domination opens up to him. Pride is not only insatiable but constantly creates situations demanding an escape to save its face. Since everything depends on his achievement he becomes too critical of what he does to complete it.)

One can scarcely avoid the contrast between the pastoral counseling approach to the division within and the approach of the *prophet of the Lord* and, consequently, of the prophetic function in the office of the ministry. This contrast, however, does not mean that either approach is in error, but rather that both have their place in the total function of the office of the ministry. The circumstances that prevail within the counseling relationship are usually not those requiring the prophetic approach. Yet there are circumstances where the prophetic approach may be demanded. In either approach the initial aim is to encourage the individual or individuals to face and assume responsibility for the basic conflict that gives rise to the destructive emotions. In instances where the prophet is required to accomplish this, his approach, if successful, may bring about a counseling relationship.

SUMMARY

From our analysis we have seen that man in his problems is a bundle of conflicts and tensions. The doctrine of man identifies the basis of these disturbances. The conflict has its source in the discrepancy between the way man was meant to be and the way he actually is. Man was created by God in his own image. Inherent in this image was the freedom to make moral choices. When man used this freedom to choose evil, his choice corrupted his inner purity, and evil, which was formerly external to him, became a part of him. Remnants of the image, however, remained, and a terrific tension developed between these two qualitative opposites in the character of man. This tension becomes increasingly unbearable as man continues to make moral decisions that manifest his corruption, and he tries to find a way of salvation. Too often his search is for an escape instead of a solution, and in running away from his problem, he not only postpones coming to grips with it, but because his way of escape is away from reality it creates a problem in itself.

In order to break up this vicious cycle of personality disintegration the doctrine of man insists that we eliminate it at its origin. Guilt must be removed to reduce the tension in the human conscience. Only then can the fellowship with God be restored that gives confidence and security to personality. In this way the destructive emotions that cause man's disintegration lose their impetus and leave him free to unite his personality around the center of life in God himself.

CHAPTER SEVEN

The Concept of the Universal Priesthood

The principles of counseling as they have developed in the clinician's laboratory are built around resources for wholeness supposedly within the counselee which respond to the counseling process. The concept of the universal priesthood describes a capacity for priesthood within the individual which is responsive to pastoral care. There is more involved, however, than a difference in terminology. The capacity for priesthood is based on the reconciliation between man and his Creator concerning the division within him. The concept of the priesthood of the believer, hence, has a prerequisite in the Creator-initiated redemption prescribed in the concept of man; there is no capacity for priesthood within the individual until there has first been a reconciliation over his rebellion against his creatureliness. So far as the theology of the church is concerned, there are no inner resources for wholeness within man until man is at peace with his God over his basic conflict between the way he is and the way he was meant to be.

SOURCES OF THE DOCTRINE

The concept of the priesthood of the believer is one of the three great doctrines stemming from the Reformation, the others being the doctrine of justification by grace through faith and the doctrine of the authority of the Scriptures. It was at the usurpation of this priesthood that Luther directed his

Treatise on the Babylonian Captivity of the Church. The doctrine itself, however, did not originate in this period of the Reformation, but is found in the writings of the fathers of both eastern and western Christendom and in Scripture itself. In fact it is in Luther's exegetical study of I Peter 2:5 that we have one of the fullest presentations of the doctrine coming out of the Reformation period.

> Come to him, to that living stone, rejected by men but in God's sight chosen and precious; and like living stones be yourselves built into a spiritual house, to be a holy priesthood, to offer spiritual sacrifices acceptable to God through Jesus Christ.

On *to be a holy priesthood*, Luther stresses the universality of this priesthood as opposed to its limitation in a clerical hierarchy or "churchy priesthood" as he called it. On *to offer spiritual sacrifices acceptable to God through Jesus Christ*, he points out the relationship of this universal priesthood to the sacrificial system of the Old Covenant.

> As to spiritual offerings, they are not money, that we must present them to the Pope; neither is the sacrifice as in the Old Testament, when men were required to sacrifice the tenth of all they had. Such outward sacrifices and priesthood have all now ceased, and all has become new and spiritual. The priest is Christ; and we all, since he has sacrificed his own body, must offer up ourselves. Here is now fulfilled all that was typified by outward sacrifices in the Old Testament, since they have all passed away, and in short all of them may be said to preach the Gospel.

Summing up the function of the believer-priest, he says:

> This is now the true priesthood, which consists in those three points as we have just heard (verse 5); namely, that we sacrifice spiritually; that we pray for the Church; and that we preach. Whoever can do this is a priest, as all are bound to be, inasmuch as they preach the word, pray for the Church, and offer themselves up before God.

In his polemical "Answer to Emser," Luther refers to his exegesis of this text as proving that all Christians are priests, "for Peter addresses all Christians, as the words themselves clearly prove and expressly mention the people by name." In this apologia he also describes the relationship between the lay and clerical priest:

> Who is priest? He who is responsible for the work and sends it forth, or the servant who carries and brings it? The priest is a messenger and servant in this work, and therefore another must be the real priest. I think this proves very clearly that we are all priests, and your priests are not a different kind of priests, but servants and officers of the common priesthood . . . and they are but workmen, servants, ministers, guardians, shepherds, keepers, and watchmen.

The relationship between the Levitical priesthood of the old covenant and the universal priesthood, referred to by Luther in his exegesis, is developed in detail in the letter to the Hebrews. The term *priest* is used contemporarily in a general sense, meaning one who functions as a leader in worship, and, specifically, as one who serves in a mediatorial capacity for the laity to the deity. The Levitical priesthood was primarily a mediatorial priesthood whose function centered in the offering of sacrifice as atonement for the sins of the people. It is in this sense also that the letter to the Hebrews portrays the priestly role of Christ and subsequently of our own priesthood through him. The ritual of the Old Testament and its fulfilment in the role of the Messiah in the New Testament is a dramatized description of the change from the spiritual childhood in the we-group of Old Testament Israel to the spiritual adulthood in the development of the individual consciousness within the church of the New Testament. The substance of the letter to the Hebrews is that the priest-role becomes internalized in personality "through faith in Christ," who brought the function of the priesthood to its completion.

For Christ has entered, not into a sanctuary made with hands, a copy of the true one, but into heaven itself, now to appear in the presence of God on our behalf. Nor was it to offer himself repeatedly, as the high priest enters the Holy Place yearly with blood not his own; for then he would have had to suffer repeatedly since the foundation of the world. But as it is, he has appeared once for all at the end of the age to put away sin by the sacrifice of himself. 9:24-26.

The close association of priesthood with sacrifice shows the necessity for a reconciliation over the division within before an individual could function as his own priest. This is illustrated by the biblical writer in his relating of the various characteristics of the Levitical mediation to the Christocentric gospel of the new covenant.

But into the second only the high priest goes, and he but once a year, and not without taking blood which he offers for himself and for the errors of the people. By this the Holy Spirit indicates that the way into the sanctuary is not yet opened as long as the outer tent is still standing (which is symbolic for the present age). 9:7-8.

This "way into the sanctuary" is the transition from the collective to the individual consciousness. It gives one the courage to affirm himself not only as a part but also as a self in relationship to God. It is effected by the redemptive act of God in Christ to heal the inner division.

Therefore, brethren, since we have confidence to enter the sanctuary by the blood of Jesus, by the new and living way which he opened for us through the curtain, that is, through his flesh, and since we have a great priest over the house of God, let us draw near with a true heart in full assurance of faith. 10:19-22.

LUTHER AND THE MEDIEVAL CHURCH

The effect of the doctrine of the priesthood of the believer on the counseling procedure is demonstrated in the difference in counseling procedure between churches who profess it and those who do not. In many ways the Roman and other

Catholic bodies have distinguished themselves in the field of pastoral counseling through the practice of auricular confession. In its espousal of the clerical over against the universal priesthood, however, the Roman Catholic practice diverges from the principles of counseling. The need for a listener and the need for confession may be satisfied through the regular practice of private confession, providing that the confession gets down to the basic problems. But when it comes to the need for understanding and the need for growth, the mediator role of the clerical priest may pose itself into the main stream of the counseling process and change its direction. In supplying the understanding and direction which his role as mediator implies, the priest may become dominant in the counseling relationship to the point of providing his help through the avenue of dependency. The need for growth, therefore, is shunted into a relationship as a part, in which the courage to be an individual is without a stimulus. The development to any advanced degree of individual consciousness with a semi-collectivist system is obviously unnecessary.

Roman Catholicism is too complex to be understood solely in terms of the mediatorship of the clergy, even in pastoral counseling. In its ascetic adherence to the Augustinian emphasis of the enjoyment of God as the chief end of man, it has produced its long line of mystics who have often transcended not only the need for clerical mediation but even the function of the priesthood of the believer, as they sought not only a person to person relationship with God but to lose themselves into the very being of God. Through such mystical experience they have developed their individual consciousness to a degree where they affirm themselves with an authority that is not so much from the group as from their own independent being. Though they retain the clerical mediation as a subjective conviction in a conventional loyalty, it has little influence in the actual character of their religious feelings.[1] It is not without significance that Luther was a member of an Augustinian order and in his turbulent struggle with his destructive emotions had explored and developed his world within. What he had found in his own mystical experiences had not seemed contrary to his medieval religious thought structure until his clash with Tetzel over a violation of spiritual values that he could scarcely dismiss. This was the initial shock that led to the conscious recognition of what had probably been heretofore unconsciously rationalized to preserve his trust in the spiritual mother to whom he had vowed his devotion. Once the break had occurred, however, he was able to disentangle his clerical mediation frame of reference from his personal religious experience and to recognize consciously the priesthood of the believer.

THE ROLE OF THE PASTOR

The doctrine of the priesthood of the believer structures by implication the role of the pastor. He is a pastor to priests. Therefore, his care in counseling or otherwise should never violate the priestly prerogatives of his people. He is to them a "servant, minister, shepherd, and watchman." As we relate this structure of the pastoral role to pastoral counseling, we make of it a means to an end rather than an end in itself. Since the pastor is not to mediate for his people but to help them to do their own mediating, pastoral counseling becomes the means to a counseling relationship with God. When this counseling relationship with the Higher Counselor is a satisfying experience for the counselee, he should have little need to continue a counseling relationship with his pastor. He becomes decreasingly dependent upon others because the coun-

[1] Cf. the works of Brother Lawrence, Bernard of Clairvaux, Gerhard Groote, Meister Eckhart, Johannes Tauler, and Francis of Assisi.

seling relationship with God is an activity within his own soul. Because of the nature of God's acceptance of the counselee, as we shall see in the chapter on sanctification, this resultant independence of others is not an antisocial withdrawal but actually leads to a new and intimate community with others.

The need for maturity, consequently, is the need for a priestly relationship with God. Counseling aims to help the counselee to help himself, that is, to help him develop his own priesthood capacities. The principles of counseling based on respect for the individual personality have their theological counterpart in the pastor's respect for the priestly potential of his counselee. And it is toward the development of this potential that his counseling activity is directed. In fact, it is precisely because people have a deficiency in their priestly function that they need and seek his help. In listening to the counselee, accepting him as he is, and recognizing his right to responsibility, the pastor is respecting his priesthood capacities and encouraging him to develop them.

AMBIVALENCE OVER THE RESPONSIBILITY OF PRIESTHOOD

In the fluctuations of daily living the priestly function of the believer may become increasingly inefficient. The press of irritation and frustration agitate the inner division, and the subsequent increase in destructive emotions may block the individual's approach to God. Although the believer has supposedly found the reconciliation for his inner division in the redemptive act of God, there is always the danger that his reconciliation may be more of an intellectual or rote acceptance than the actual *credo* of his total person. The manner in which the individual meets the problems of the hour reveals the depth of this reconciliation, for if the negative feelings of guilt and fear and resentment are not effectively dispersed, they pose as a threat to his security, and consequently may move him to reinforce his ego-center which in turn will isolate him even further from communion with others, including God. He needs his pastor to help him remove this block to his priestly relationship with God.

Even though such individuals feel hindered in their direct approach to God and seek the pastor's help in this problem, they may be ambivalent over the desire for their own mediatorship. It requires a responsibility they may not be willing to assume. There is a resistance toward maturity even as there is a desire for it. The same individual may have a fear of freedom as well as a longing for it. At the same moment the counselee is determined to break out of his rut, he is also determined to stay in it. The negative feelings provide their own resistance to their elimination; the disintegration in personality that they create is most clearly revealed to the counselee as he struggles in the counseling process to overcome them. One becomes accustomed to his misery and though he longs to be without it he is in a sense at home with it. There is a certain fear of leaving home—an apprehension toward life in a foreign land. There is also a sense of guilt in the thought of no longer enduring a slavery which has perhaps had its compensations in self-atonement. As such a person would step across the threshold into freedom he would upset whatever semblance of equilibrium he has maintained and the resultant anxiety may cause him to retreat to the pseudo-security of his ego-center.

As a consequence, the counselee may sabotage his own progress by tempting the pastor to assume his mediatorial role for him. Unfortunately, there is no insurance against a pastor assuming the role of priest simply because he is a Protestant minister. The predisposition to assume mediatorial powers for another is as frequently of psychological origin as of theological indoctrination. Even as there is a fear of assuming the responsibility of priesthood oneself, so there is a fear of allotting to others this same responsibility. It takes a counselor who has himself experienced the independence of priesthood to lead a counselee into this same maturity. Because of the pastor's apprehensions over his own adequacy as a counselor, he needs a strong faith in the doctrine of the priesthood of the believer, both to recognize the temptation in the counselee's invitation and to resist it. He faces this same danger when whatever apparent success he has as a counselor leads him to an overconfidence in his authority as an expert.

Should he succumb from either of these reasons to this temptation to mediate, he will either incite immediate or ultimate resistance from the counselee as a violation of his own priestly prerogatives or he will have him yielding to this mediatorship as an escape from maturity. Even though the counselee asks for his mediation, the opposite and overshadowed pole of his ambivalence receives its impetus to rebel when such mediation is actually assumed. When there is no such resistance it may mean that his desire for maturity has been repressed sufficiently to insure his dependency.

I have been reminded of this the hard way. Because she was timid and suspicious and had difficulty expressing herself, Mrs. Ross was not an easy person to counsel. She was worried about the impression she was making on me, but I felt it was I myself who was on trial. Evidently I betrayed my concern as I wracked my brain to figure out a way to help her, for she interrupted my efforts to say, "You make me feel so guilty. You seem to be working so much harder on my problem than I am." It was the reprimand I needed to get out of her territory.

Even those who are outwardly rebellious against any mediator may be inwardly fearful of assuming the responsibility for their own mediation. They are equally as fixed in their immaturity as in their rebellion. Resistance to pastoral mediation is not in itself the courage to be an individual. It may simply be resistance to a domination which the person has learned to resent, but which he is unable to assume himself, largely because his experience with this domination has inhibited the development of his confidence in himself, and because his creative energies have turned into negative or resistant movements as a result of this encroachment. Secretly he feels the need for somebody to assume his responsibilities but his resistance end of the ambivalence is too strong to allow this desire any external expression. Because of its uncoercive and yet understanding nature, a counseling relationship structured on the concept of the universal priesthood will usually bring this ambivalence to the surface.

Ben Robertson had always been "as independent as a hog on ice." Flaunting the mores of his group was nothing new for him, but this time his defiance of the rules got him into more of a scrape than he anticipated, and the intensity of the community censure began to get him down. Since his pastor had always respected Ben's individuality, he had Ben's respect in return, and in trouble Ben came to him. It took some time for him to air his grievances but because his right to his feelings was accepted he was able to face a painful reality.

BEN: Why don't people let a person lead his own life? What business is it of theirs if I don't choose to live like they think I should? But they make it their business and so I'm over a barrel.

PASTOR: You resent their opinions and yet can't get away from them.

BEN: No, darn it. You've got to live with them. (pause) I don't imagine anybody likes the idea of being blackballed.

PASTOR: What people think of us does make a difference to us.

BEN: I hate to admit it.

PASTOR: Sure, I understand.

BEN: You like to think of yourself with some sort of standing. Not so much whether they approve of you or not—but that they at least think you've got something on the ball.

Because they are set in their indifference, people like Ben change slowly. To admit he was dependent upon those whom he had boasted that he cared nothing about was a significant step in his progress.

So it is that the doctrine of the priesthood of the believer describes a great democracy in the area of the spirit. As such it is an outgrowth of the concept of the *imago Dei* as it is structured in the doctrine of man. Even as our century has witnessed repeatedly how a people will abandon their democratic form of government in a trade for the security of a "fuehrer" when the going gets tough, so individuals may allow others to take the responsibility for the direction of their lives when they feel unable to do it themselves. They exchange their freedom as individual priests for the security that comes from having another mediate for them.

There are people who use "counseling" as a crutch. The relief they receive through catharsis is enough to sustain them until the next appointment. They may even be helped by advice concerning the surface manifestations of the basic problem. Yet they stay on the surface because they lack the courage to go deeper, being afraid of what they will see and of what they will have to do. In this sense they are also using "counseling" as an escape—hoping the pastor will do for them what they have to do for themselves. Counseling that is structured on the basis of the universal priesthood cannot be exploited in this manner. Either the counselee allows it to take him deeper, or, realizing he cannot switch the responsibility to the counselor, he loses interest.

Mr. Thorp was besieged by periods of anxiety and depression during which times he would keep his whole family in a dither. He was quite amenable to his wife's suggestion that he see the pastor, and during his interviews with him showed considerable insight into the nature of his problem. But nothing seemed to change. Each time Mr. Thorp would return in the picture of despair. On one occasion the pastor's response brought things to a head.

THORP: Nothing seems to work. Maybe there isn't any use. I don't suppose anybody can help me. I feel like giving up.

PASTOR: You feel there is nothing that can be done for you.

THORP: (Looking rather startled) Don't *you* think there is?

PASTOR: My thoughts in the matter are based on how *you* feel about it, Mr. Thorp, because it is how you feel about it that determines whether anything can be done or not.

THORP: Well—ah—I naturally have some hope—otherwise I wouldn't be here.

While there was no radical improvement, there was a definite change in Mr. Thorp's co-operation from this point on. By his defeated attitude he was trying to shift the responsibility for his improvement to the pastor. When he realized the pastor's convictions made this impossible, he quickly saw that he had to change his approach—or end the interviews, which he did not want to do.

Even as the individualistic spirit is often succeeded by the rise of the paternalistic state, so the individual who ultimately despairs of making any meaning out of his life for himself will find refuge in a kind of spiritual childhood—in a religious leader or group who as a spiritual parent is the mediator of the *Purpose*. This paternal assurance stills the anxiety of emptiness and the threat of nonbeing. If this new security proves insufficient in itself to disperse his anxiety, the individual may take the succeeding step into idolatry. In this manner the threats within are transferred to an outer enemy, not merely of oneself but of the group and its leader. The inner agitation is then channeled in fanatical attack on this common enemy.[2]

CLIMAX IN THE DEVOTIONAL LIFE

When the pastor follows his role in counseling as it is structured by the doctrine of the universal priesthood, the result of his counseling would prepare the way for a counseling relationship with God. This same structure of the pastoral role is being emphasized also in the related field of preaching. In their modification for pulpit use, the principles of counseling as they are embodied in this doctrine, offer the preacher an approach in leading his hearers to the spiritual sensitivity in which God and they can meet in the divine-human encounter.[3] This same structure holds also for the teaching ministry. As important as indoctrination may be in religious education, even indoctrination concerning the priesthood of the believer, the aim of teaching goes beyond indoctrination to the stimulation of the person-to-person experience with God. The devotional life of God's people is the inescapable climax to the various functions of the office of the ministry as they are patterned after the doctrine of the priesthood of the believer.

Although the cultivation of the devotional life is an area of pastoral care in itself, it cannot be separated from the counseling process when it is involved in the counseling relationship.

[2] For two distinct analyses of idolatry see Fritz Kunkel, *op. cit.*, Chapter 6, and Paul Ramsey, *Basic Christian Ethics* (New York: Scribners, 1951), p. 295-306.

[3] This is Bishop Gerald Kennedy's emphasis in his *Word Through Preaching*.

The principles of counseling as they are oriented in the doctrine of the universal priesthood pertain also to this pastoral ministry to the devotional life. Each believer is not only a priest but a unique priest. The characteristics of the individual personality determine the manner in which one will exercise his priesthood. The priesthood doctrine allows for this variation in the devotional life: the counselee is helped to discover the way in which he can most effectively commune with God.

The disregard of the implication of the priesthood doctrine for the devotional life has created its divisions within the church. Men have failed to recognize as an adiaphoron the manner of approach in one's encounter with God and have placed a premium on their own particular experience or the accepted practice of their group and have frowned on the variations of others. The counselee will be stimulated to greater religious growth if he follows a devotional procedure in line with his personality traits rather than in opposition to them.

People with personality problems often develop in a more vertical manner than the apparently adjusted person whose life extends more in a horizontal direction toward his neighbors. Feeling somewhat out of the group, they live within themselves, and the pain of their inner conflicts has a deepening effect on the character of their thoughts. To direct them into a devotional procedure adapted to personality patterns of the horizontal nature would not satisfy their priestly needs. They would be more inclined to adopt a procedure that would fit in with their characteristic way of behavior—that would match the vertical nature of their thinking and of their feeling in their world within. Usually it is the more contemplative type of devotional practice that most adequately meets these needs. We will explore this subject further in the chapter on the use of the means of grace in counseling. It suffices to say that it is the counselee priest who must determine the procedure of most value to him.

It should be obvious that the principles of counseling do not have to become religious to adapt to pastoral counseling; they are already religious. As Wise has pointed out, God does not have to be brought into the counseling process; he is already there.[4] As these principles form the basis for the role of the counselor in terms of the doctrine of the universal priesthood, they demonstrate the approach of God. In the permissive relationship with the counselor which encourages the growth of the counselee there are present those qualities of divinity which God himself manifests in his own counseling relationships. That God works through human relationships is the theological foundation to the office of the ministry.

It does not follow, as Wise seems to intimate, that because God is manifest in the dynamic of the counseling relationship that there is no specific value in the mention of his name. Or that specific reference to any religious doctrine is superfluous. The educative role of the pastor is not dissociated from the counseling process, particularly after the initial stages of the relationship. During this time the mention of God, of religious doctrine and practice, may be of decided advantage in the process toward maturity.

SUMMARY

In acknowledging the priestly capacity within the believer, the doctrine of the universal priesthood presupposes its own solution, the mediatorship of Christ, to the fundamental conflict in man as described in the corruption of the *imago Dei*. From the point of view of the theology of the church it is doubtful if one can rely on any inner potential for wholeness unless there has first been an inner reconciliation between man

[4] Carroll Wise, *op. cit.*, p. 154.

and God. With this proviso the counselor's objective of helping the counselee help himself is identical with the pastor's objective of helping the believer develop his own priestly capacities.

The doctrine of the priesthood of the believer outlines the role of the pastor as a counselor. As a pastor to priests his task is a means to an end; the purpose of his counseling is to lead his counselee to the Higher Counselor. People with problems often have difficulty in contacting the Higher Counselor. They come to the pastor because of this deficiency. His great temptation is to try to hurry the process along by stepping outside of his pastoral role in an attempt to double for the Higher Counselor. When he yields to this temptation the counseling process becomes a hindrance rather than an incentive to maturity. As the priestly function of the counselee becomes blocked, the pastor's task is not to jump in and mediate for him, but to remove the block so that he may resume his own mediatorship. The need for maturity therefore is the need for a priestly relationship with God. The goal of the believer is to become increasingly conscious of the presence of God so that he may commune with him and know his mind and his purposes.

CHAPTER EIGHT

The Concept of Freedom

"The point of most intimate conflict between secular and pastoral viewpoints concerns the relation of sin and maladjustment. Scientific counseling seeks to avoid moralism and judgmentalisms, and does not concern itself with questions of sin,"[1] Thorne states. Prominent among the reasons that the secular counselor may give for rejecting "moralism and judgmentalisms" would be that such may lead to the repression rather than to the solution of conflict. Any approach encouraging repression would be out of harmony with the principles of counseling. It would be opposed also by the theology of the church. In the concept of Christian liberty this theology rejects the legalism implied in Thorne's "moralism and judgmentalisms." As so often happens, however, it is this legalistic interpretation of conduct that is associated with the heritage of the church rather than a freedom from law. This is the freedom that develops from the priesthood of the believer. When one lacks the courage to affirm this freedom as his own, he becomes a natural candidate for the "bondage of the law."

Although Luther's *The Freedom of the Christian Man* is the classical work on the concept of Christian liberty, the most concise formulation for our purpose is in Calvin's *Insti-*

[1] Frederick C. Thorne, *op. cit.*, p. 481.

tutes. In line with his gift for the systematic, Calvin divides the doctrine into three parts.

1. The first part is that consciences of believers, when seeking an assurance of their justification before God, should raise themselves above the law, and forget all the righteousness of the law.

2. The second part of Christian liberty, which is dependent on the first, is, that their consciences do not observe the law as being under any legal obligations; but that, being liberated from the yoke of the law, they yield a voluntary obedience to the will of God.

3. The third part of Christian liberty teaches us, that we are bound by no obligation before God respecting external things, which in themselves are indifferent; but that we may indifferently sometimes use, and at other times omit them.

According to the first part, the conscience of a Christian, released from all guilt associated with unrighteousness, is above any operation by law. In the second, the individual with a conscience so liberated is able to associate himself voluntarily with "the will of God." He is also not obligated, according to part three, to follow any set practice of observable piety, but may decide on the basis of the immediate situation to use or not use these "external things." It may appear incongruous to associate Calvin with Christian liberty, considering his role in the experiment at Geneva. Though he was apparently attracted toward legalism in practice, intellectually Calvin was committed to the Reformation spirit of freedom through maturity.

LEGALISM VS. CHRISTIANITY

The battle against legalism within religion is about as old as religion itself. Wherever there is a systematization of religious thought and practice, there also is the danger of using the system apart from the spirit it was meant to express. In its more rudimentary stage the conflict is apparent even within the covenant of law in the Old Testament period. The prophet of the Lord rose up in times of decadence to challenge the dissociation of conformity with spirit in the observance of priestly ritual. "I will have mercy and not sacrifice," is the radical criterion of a religion of motive.

So far as Christian theology is concerned, however, the conflict between liberty and legalism is climaxed in the conflict between Christ and the Pharisees. Law in the redemptive work of the Messiah is not only inseparable from motive, it is transcended entirely. It was not that Jesus wanted to show that laws must be set aside for humanitarian emergencies; the Pharisees believed this. Nor that there must be a distinction between avoidable and unavoidable work on the Sabbath: the Pharisees also believed this. It was not that the Pharisees' multiplication of laws and fences made it more difficult for the people to follow their righteousness; in fact it made it easier. Jesus was not trying to show that some laws were more fundamental than others. Hillel had done that already. His message was that the kingdom of God was not concerned with observing laws at all.[2]

This clash between the Pharisaical culture and the Messianic gospel is illustrated in the interview between Jesus and Nicodemus. When Jesus told Nicodemus that except he be born anew he could not see the kingdom of God, Nicodemus could not even understand what Jesus was talking about. Christ was showing that there is no continuity between the old and the new, between the natural and the spiritual, between the thought forms of Nicodemus and those of Jesus. When Nicodemus asked if he must enter again his mother's womb to achieve this rebirth, he showed how little sense he saw in what Jesus was saying. Here was not necessarily a

[2] For a penetrating analysis of Jesus' conflict with the Pharisees, see Paul Ramsey, *op. cit.*, pp. 46-74.

conflict between good and evil men, but between two radically different points of view in regard to religious and moral conduct.

The great gulf between the thought forms of Nicodemus and those of Jesus continued into the apostolic church in the conflict between St. Paul and the Judaizers. These Hebrew "converts" to Christ who wanted to retain the ceremonial structure of the old covenant within the framework of the new covenant were not merely conservatives acting as a healthy caution on any rapid change. They were those who would put the new wine in old wineskins; unconsciously perhaps but indubitably they were opposing the gospel, and the wine would be spilled. It is to the credit of St. Paul that he saw clearly into the issues involved and exposed the Judaistic movement for what it was. Because of his uncompromising stand, the church was forced to face this conflict and to make its decision. In what was apparently the first church convention this doctrinal dispute was given its public hearing and the result was a decided victory for the liberty of the new covenant. The rent that might have destroyed the essence of the Messianic covenant at its beginning was officially mended.

Despite the clarity of the Jerusalem decision, the Judaistic controversy was not dead. Like all legalisms, its origin was predominantly psychological, and the personality structure of the Judaizer was not likely to be changed by a church vote. Paul's letter to the Galatians is a later and more drastic attempt to counteract a renewed outbreak of this threat. Here the apostle labels the legalistic emphasis a "different gospel." If righteousness comes by the law—any and all laws—then Christ died for naught. Moralism and judgmentalisms "frustrate the grace of God." To return to a covenant of law is to go from the position of an heir who has come into his possession, to one who is yet a child and "no better than a slave." It is to return to the "weak and beggarly elemental spirits"—to surrender to a "yoke of slavery."

The conflict with the Judaizers passed from the scene with the eclipse of Jewish influence at the close of the first century. The controversy between liberty and legalism, however, continued. It broke out in an entirely different pattern in the historic Augustine-Pelagius clash in the fourth century. At first glance it may appear that Augustine in his doctrine of total depravity is destroying the humanist appeal in the structure of the kingdom and that Pelagius with his doctrine of moral neutrality gives incentive to any human effort for good. It is only as both interpretations of human nature are allowed to work themselves out in the history of personality that Pelagius turns out to be the legalist and Augustine the liberator.

In recognizing natural man's moral bankruptcy the Augustinian emphasis leads one to surrender all attempts to justify himself on the basis of righteousness and to give himself up to the mercy of God. This is the frame of mind, as we shall see in later chapters, that is receptive to divine grace and to the rebirth which Jesus said was fundamental to salvation. The Pelagian point of view relies on man's will power for the development of his morality. The very struggle that the will must put forth to accomplish this righteousness betrays the presence of an opposing will within. In the words of Augustine's predecessor, "So I find it to be a law that when I want to do right, evil lies close at hand. For I delight in the law of God, in my inmost self, but I see in my members another law at war with the law of my mind and making me captive to the law of sin which dwells in my members." [8] Whatever victory will power would gain would be an "in spite of" victory. Its "clear-cutness" would be only in the peripheral

[8] Romans 7:21-23.

area of personality that is observable through external activity. This tends to shift the center of this achievable morality from the inner struggle to the outer manifestation in order to preserve the Pelagian presupposition. Hence we arrive at the legalistic position. To illustrate: I have a selfish thought. By my will power I can shut this thought off. I can keep it from carrying itself into its corresponding selfish action. I can even create what looks like an unselfish thought and carry it out into what looks like an unselfish action. I cannot, however, by my will power cease being selfish. My only recourse in maintaining my belief in righteousness by will power is to use my will power to repress the "shadow." [4] And so I return to the moralism and judgmentalisms condemned by the principles of counseling.

The Pelagian point of view, however, can serve a good purpose if when it proves itself inadequate it leads to conscious defeat rather than unconscious repression. It may take a thoroughgoing attempt as a Pelagian before one can really arrive at the Augustinian position. This is the route by which the alcoholic becomes redeemable in the program of Alcoholics Anonymous. In a modified way it is the route also by which Luther arrived at the experience that gave birth to the Reformation.

LEGALISM AND SELF-DECEPTION

Both the Augustinian and Pelagian positions are reactions to the ominous appearances of determinism in moral conduct. The Pelagian idea is a complete denial of this determinism while the Augustinian position is an acknowledgment of it for the purpose of altering it. The powerfully determining factors of heredity and environment are adequately provided

[4] This is Jung's term for the conflict within that threatens the ego-center.

for in the Augustinian emphasis. If there is an ego appeal in affirming a freedom one does not have, there is also such an appeal in denying all responsibility for one's predicament. The Augustinian emphasis avoids this pitfall by insisting upon individual responsibility in spite of overpowering influences, both because the individual concurs in his immoral decisions and because there is something that can be done about it. The purpose of such a teaching is not to produce a remorse in despair but a repentance in hope. It brings us to the realization of our own insufficiency (finitude) that we may look beyond ourselves to the sufficiency (infinitude) of God. In the one emphasis the individual defies determinism by repression and in the other he defies it by "giving up to God."

The success of legalism depends upon keeping one's motives buried. The emphasis on overt behavior is an emphasis on the *seen* and consequently on the observer. This dependency upon the approval of at least certain others prevents the development of individual consciousness because the security derived thereby depends upon a self-affirmation at the expense of reality. In this manner legalism becomes a neurosis—a method of defense for the ego center. The shadow is both the true motive which keeps threatening to break out of the unconscious to discredit the behavior and the destructive emotions that operate in opposition to the overt act.

Even as there is a certain collectivism in the security of the legalist, so there is also a disruption of any group solidarity in egocentricity. Guilt repressed may seek its outlet in the condemnation of others. Even as he needs like-minded people to support his ego defense, so the legalist needs a scapegoat to absorb his inner agitation. Because of the rigidity of his obedience to his laws and the intensity of his attack on the disobedient, the legalist gives an appearance of strength which often evokes both fear and respect from the onlookers. The precarious picture of his inner equilibrium, however, reveals him as the "weaker brother." [5]

This tendency to center evil as such in the external leads to an overbalance in the direction of the body. The sins that can be most completely controlled by will power are those associated with the physical appetites. The result is that legalism goes hand in hand with the Platonic concept of values. When evil is associated primarily with the physical, the ready affinity of sexual power for guilt is exploited. It is of interest that not only in the semi-Pelagianism of Roman Catholicism is there an exaltation of virginity, but also in the more legalistic circles in the history of Calvinism there has been almost a condemnation of sexual manifestation as a whole. Thus it is evident that no mere subscription to Augustinian total depravity will guarantee the avoidance of legalism. The subscription itself can become a legalism and hence unable to channel the creative powers inherent in its doctrinal picture.

In the Pauline concept of the works of the flesh, the so-called sins of the body are outnumbered in the catalogue by the sins of the spirit. The *sarx* of New Testament theology is the corruption of the image of God in the soul, and consequently a rejection of the Platonic association of virtue with spirit. That expert in satanic psychology, C. S. Lewis, designates the sins of the body as the animal self and the sins of the spirit as the diabolical self. The devil, says Lewis, is more than eager to assist us in overcoming the animal self if he can stimulate the diabolical self in the bargain.[6]

The "miracle" of counseling, with its history in Freudian discoveries, is the unearthing of repressions often caused by these distorted concepts of Christian virtue. Based on principles opposite to those leading to repression, the purpose of

[5] I Corinthians 8:7.
[6] C. S. Lewis, *Christian Behaviour* (New York: Macmillan, 1943), p. 29.

counseling is not only to release the repression but to remedy the cause. Because a person's religion is at stake when these religiously caused repressions are unearthed, it is better for the future religious development of the counselee if the counseling that liberates him is religiously oriented rather than of secular nature.

CHRISTIAN LIBERTY AND SELF-UNDERSTANDING

What appears to be at the heart of the problem is the inner conflict in man that creates the impression of determinism toward evil. The only apparent freedom would be freedom from this inner conflict with its resultant bondage to the destructive emotions. Repression of the negative end of this conflict has been explored and found wanting. Since repression is not elimination but simply unconscious deception, it throws the personality off center, and in this state of disintegration no individual is able to unite his energies in any one direction. The accompanying distortion in perspective that his being off-center creates increases the disintegration and its resultant maladjustment to environment. The result of repression as a way to freedom is a greater enslavement to the destructive emotions.

If repression of the negative is no solution to this conflict, then how about a free expression of the negative? If it is the conflict between motive and deed, between destructive feelings and conscience, between natural desires and cultural standards, that locks a man in conflict, then would he not find freedom in the free expression of his natural self? The hitch is that this conflict is not between the individual and his environment. Regardless of how we may account for this conflict through the influence of heredity or environment, his conflict is now his own. It is within him and as much a part of him as any other influence which has been incorporated into the development of his personality. To give free expression to what the legalist would repress would only change the complexion of the conflict. His expression could not be free because the positive opposite of his expression is also within him. The result would either be increased guilt or a repression of the "positive pole." In addition, the free expression of hitherto repressed desires and feelings would in all probability curtail this same freedom in others and lead to increased maladjustment to group living. The way to freedom, hence, cannot come from a denial of either of the qualitative opposites in the soul of man but from a resolution of these opposites into an integrated approach to life. The doctrine of Christian liberty proposes to effect such an integration through its "voluntary obedience to the will of God."

Christian liberty is the expression of self-fulfilment that comes from finding the true center for living, in contrast to the self-destructive "kicking against the pricks" of living off-center. It is a freedom that is realized through a co-operation with, rather than a rebellion against, the creative process of life—the will of God. Because its moral analysis is centered in the realm of motives we can speak of it as "depth morality" —the theological counterpart to depth psychology. According to this depth morality one must accept himself before he can overcome his enslavement to evil. As a reaction to the division within, such self-acceptance is the opposite of repression, and is preceded by the courage to face the shadow, in contrast to the fear that seeks only an escape. The basis for this courage is faith. By means of this faith, one is able to counteract the defensive impulse to repress his ambivalence, because he is able to recognize the uncontrollable without anxiety and to face the inner evil without depression. The need for confession in the light of the doctrine of Christian liberty would be the need to unearth the repressed and to prevent further repression.

The doctrine obviously builds upon something that stimulates such a faith. This *something* is the redemptive gospel that God's acceptance (justification) of the individual is not contingent upon the elimination of his inner division. Luther in his *Freedom of the Christian Man* says:

> Since then, works justify no one, and a man must be righteous before he does a good work, it is very evident that it is faith alone, which, because of the pure mercy of God through Christ and in His Word, worthily and sufficiently justifies and saves the person, and a Christian man has no need of any work or any law in order to be saved, since through faith he is free from every law and does all that he does out of pure liberty and freely, seeking neither benefit nor salvation, since he already abounds in all things and is saved through the grace of God because of his faith and now seeks only to please God.

This is the "prior assurance of salvation" that liberates one from the fear of rejection, so that he can do what he does as a free man. We will take up the nature of God's acceptance in the next chapter. Our purpose here is to note the effects of this acceptance in the moral nature of man. Obedience to the will of God, we see, is not conformity to "God's laws" but an attitude or direction of personality called "faith" that results from the experience of divine acceptance.

In view of the nature of human existence, human freedom is not exercised explicitly in doing the will of God nor in doing as one pleases, but in desiring to do the will of God. It is not only outward actions that must be in line with the creative process in life, but the motives as well. Freedom, consequently, has to operate beyond the law or it is not freedom. While it may be contended that the law is not necessarily a control from without but that there is a certain natural law in the makeup of man, it is not so much the source of the law that disqualifies its influence for freedom but the nature of law itself. Freedom is more than even self-regulation. The stimulus for the type of self-regulation that would be tantamount to freedom would have to be capable of more spontaneity than any law—even natural law—could engender. To overcome the conflict within personality to the extent necessary for the experience of Christian liberty—and self-regulation without conflict—one would have to be motivated in his whole person by a dynamic pull. The only power capable of integrating both the inner motive and the outer behavior around the will of God, according to the doctrine, is love. Not, do as you will, but love and then do as you will.

Love is a total response of personality in which the positive polarity of the emotions is dominant. Love, therefore, is the true center for living. It is a psychic energy that only something capable of a mutual response can evoke. Hence the inadequacy of a "lifeless law" to elicit a total response from personality. Love as the true center liberates one from the bondage of distortion in the perspective inherent in the off-center. Morally speaking, this means freedom from a peripheral and atomistic view of good and evil that is the automatic outcome of the imbalance toward the external that characterizes the off-center. The perspective of the true center focuses on the essence of righteousness and of evil; it is the motive of love that determines righteous conduct and its opposite, pride, that is at the source of evil. This love, according to St. Paul in his Galatian epistle, is directed toward the "neighbor" and is the realization of all that the law had structured.

> For the whole law is fulfilled in one word, "You shall love your neighbor as yourself."

In this focus on love and pride, the Christian is freed from subservience to "external things" to deal with the essentials.

His rigid straining at the gnats—the marks of piety divorced from the consideration of motive—is broken to prevent his swallowing the camel—his oblivion to the weightier matters of motive. The need for understanding in terms of Christian liberty is the need to understand one's motives. Bondage and freedom are identified in terms of evil in its essence and righteousness in its essence. Love is the only antidote strong enough to heal the disunity in personality created, perpetuated and aggravated by pride. Under its dynamic the destructive emotions are converted into the creative emotions that are in line with the will of God in life. Christian liberty is the "faith working through love" process of Christian ethics, whose radical emphasis on motive is most conclusively enunciated in St. Paul's ode to Christian love, where he states that even in the extremities of obvious self-denial—giving up all material possessions and offering my body as a martyr—except they be done out of love, "I gain nothing."

In its processes of honesty through confession and understanding through acceptance, this discipline of depth morality effects the recognition of natural talents and interests which otherwise might be hidden in the confusion or buried in the repression of a house divided against itself. The individual who begins to experience the liberation in this discipline is free not only to understand himself but to *be* himself. With the necessity for a facade no longer present, he can develop his personality and plan for his future in harmony with the unique nature of his being. This illustrates the direct correlation between freedom and self-fulfilment: without the former the latter would be beyond actualization and without the latter the former would be an illusion.

Sandra Marks was arrested on a morals charge and probated to her pastor. During their first counseling interview she was embarrassed because of what she had done but could not explain why she had gotten herself into this predicament. The pastor encouraged her to recall any possible clues from her earlier life that might have a bearing on her present situation. With considerable hesitancy she related incidents of childhood sex play, its discovery by the parents, and the vivid impression of guilt left by the experience. As she went into this and later pre-adolescent sexual experimentation, Sandra was under a noticeable strain. It was obvious that she would not choose to talk about these things, nor would she have come to her pastor on her own. When she returned the pastor asked her if any other insights had come to her during the week. She said, "I've been pretty busy—I haven't done much thinking about it. It's better that way, isn't it? I've heard it's best to keep your mind occupied so you don't think about these things."

In the counseling room she could not escape. At length she was led to the great trauma in her life, as with considerable emotion and reluctance, she told of her love for her father, of the divorce, and of her separation from her father. He was the one person in her life with whom she had a secure relationship, and her grief over his loss was antagonized by the injustice of it. Her loneliness was intensely painful. When she had gotten it all out, this is what happened:

PASTOR: It seems like it was just yesterday, doesn't it?

SANDRA: There are chills going up and down my back.

And later:

SANDRA: When I began going with a fellow, I was afraid I'd lose him. I think that's why I started getting in trouble—I wanted to be sure it wouldn't happen again.

PASTOR: You wanted a tie that couldn't be broken.

SANDRA: I knew it was wrong. But when you need something real bad, that doesn't seem so important.

After this she became more relaxed. In succeeding interviews she talked quite freely about things that had previously made her most uneasy. When the pastor commented on this, Sandra said, "I know. I actually felt good when I left here the last time. And that's something compared to the way it was at first."

In understanding why she had gotten into her trouble Sandra felt more secure in overcoming her problem, something the fear of losing her probation could not do for her. Grief needs to be talked out to heal.

When a counselee is "under the law," he is afraid to face himself. If the spirit of the gospel can be introduced through the pastoral relationship, he may be encouraged to look within himself. At first what he sees will be repugnant to him, but when he is aware that the pastor accepts him nevertheless, his aversion gives way to acceptance. By giving expression to the dark things within, he will understand why as well as what. The result is more self-acceptance since self-understanding leads to self-forgiveness. The outcome is a liberation, like the opening of the prison which the prophet said would happen when the gospel is received.

> The Spirit of the Lord God is upon me,
> because the Lord has anointed me
> to bring good tidings to the afflicted;
> he has sent me to bind up the brokenhearted,
> to proclaim liberty to the captives,
> and the opening of the prison to those who are bound.[7]

Those who are under bondage to the law may try to escape its condemnation in some roundabout way. Carl Smith got into an argument with his pastor during the Bible class, maintaining that man was a predestined creature in all his ways. Half an hour later he was still at it with his pastor alone.

[7] Isaiah 61:1.

Having given all the answers he knew, the pastor became convinced that Carl did not want to change his mind, even though he was not satisfied with his own conclusions.

Here is part of the discussion.

PASTOR: Carl, why is this such a problem to you?

CARL: I find myself wanting to dispute this love of God you talk about.

PASTOR: You feel a resistance toward it.

CARL: If it is true that God's love is so wonderful, then the opposite is also true.

PASTOR: And what is that?

CARL: The condemnation. My own responsibility.

PASTOR: You feel you are failing somewhere along the line.

CARL: Everything about me. I get so discouraged trying to climb out of the hole only to keep falling back in.

PASTOR: You are trying to overcome something, but not succeeding.

CARL: I don't want to go into it—it's just me.

The following interview Carl came to the point.

CARL: I've been taking things—and money. I don't know why. I really don't. It's all been just small stuff.

PASTOR: There's a reason for it, but you don't know what it is.

CARL: I suppose that's about it.

PASTOR: If you would like we could work at it together, Carl. When you find out why you do it, I'm sure you will be able to do something about stopping it.

CARL: It has helped me so much to see why I hated to hear about God's love—and, incidently, hated you for defending it so well. If I could just get this other thing cleared up the same way—it would be wonderful.

NEIGHBOR LOVE AND MATURITY

Neighbor love as a self-regulated dynamic from within enhances individual responsibility. In this manner the need for maturity is realized in terms of one's union with the group. So far as the doctrine of Christian liberty is concerned there could be no growth in individuality apart from a growth in oneness with one's fellows. In loving his neighbor as himself, one, as it were, would love himself in his neighbor. If we invert this equation as Luther suggested, the Christian would love himself as he loves his neighbor. The projection of the self into the neighbor and into God is to Luther the meaning of "faith working through love."

> A Christian man lives not in himself but in Christ and his neighbor. Otherwise he is not a Christian. He lives in Christ through faith, in his neighbor through love; by faith he is caught up beyond himself into God, by love he sinks down beneath himself into his neighbor.[8]

The emphasis upon union with the group should not leave the impression that such union is identical with harmonious relations with the group. Social maladjustment is an arbitrary term and too often is applied indiscriminately to the activities of any individual who may be disruptive to the peace of society. Maladjustment in this sense may also be the mark of the freedom through maturity. Love is not synonymous with being nice or with being agreeable. In fact, love may and often does demand the opposite. An uncompromising protest may be far more needful to a group on occasion than a congenial spirit encouraging a complacency that may lead to ruin. People may fear to differ because it threatens their security. Only maladjustment caused by egocentricity is maladjustment in its usual context of mental ill-health. Again

[8] Martin Luther, "Treatise on Christian Liberty," *Works of Martin Luther*, Holman Edition (1916), II, p. 342.

it is to the motive that the doctrine of Christian liberty directs us in diagnosing the social maturity of the individual.

Although both from a social and individual point of view the doctrine of Christian liberty is the doctrine of self-fulfilment, it is neighbor love with its background of faith and not the drive for self-fulfilment that is the way of achieving this self-fulfilment. How now to achieve this love? Here is the enigma of a psychology without God, of the principles of counseling without religion. It is to theological concepts that take us beyond the realm of psychology that we must turn for an answer—doctrines that describe the nature of God and his redemption of man.

SUMMARY

The doctrine of Christian liberty has as its initial premise the belief that a person must face the evil within him and not repress it. To meet the need of the counselee to understand his problem this doctrine bids him look within himself to his motives. It is not only what a man does or does not do that is important but also why he does it. The counselee cannot evaluate his activities without knowing the motives behind them. Yet it is these very motives that he would like to ignore. Although what we see when we examine our motives may depress us, we may as well know the truth. The only way to change reality is first of all to accept it. After we accept ourselves as sinners—even as God does—we can begin to understand ourselves.

When we look at our motives we see that the basis of man's sin is his pride. It builds up a wall between him and his fellow-man and makes him a competitor with God. We also see that righteousness centers in love. As the opposite of pride love breaks down our wall of egocentricity and joins us in a spirit of union with our neighbors. The only way for a person to unify himself and become free is to bring both his motives and his activities in line with the will of God. It is love that can make this possible. It enables him actually to want to do the will of God. Love, hence, is both the goal and the dynamic of the doctrine of Christian liberty. It is freedom in its deepest meaning.

CHAPTER NINE

The Means of Acceptance

There may be the objection that in the doctrines now before us we are leaving the area of counseling resources and entering those of homiletics and religious education. These are the doctrines, however, that undergirded the pastoral counseling process for centuries. To exclude them upon the basis of definition is an arbitrary limitation to what is meant by pastoral counseling. In fact there is a sense in which these resources can be said to make the difference between counseling and pastoral counseling. While it is correct that God is revealed in human processes and, in particular, in the processes of the counseling relationship as they are based on the principles of counseling, he is more than these processes. God, like theology, can neither be separated from the dynamics of human experience nor reduced to symbols as psychological phenomena. He can become so immanent in our interpretation of his role in human processes that he may become identical with them.

This is exactly what has happened in the growing movement of religious humanism that dispenses with the transcendency of God, especially, for our interest, that religious humanism based upon the science of depth psychology. Not only is the transcendency of God considered inconsequential, but the immanence of God is indistinguishable from subjective religion. Fromm, for example, develops this idea of God working through human processes as they are revealed through psychoanalysis and then bluntly asks why in our present advance in human evolution we need any longer retain the symbol, *God.* Yet in dispensing with the symbol, *God,* Fromm in his religious humanism confesses a faith that is as biblical if not more so than the credo of the worshipers of the immanent God. He insists upon an absolute in ethics and in truth, the centrality of *God* as love, the disintegrating effect of all idolatry, and the religious necessity for social consciousness.

We have in this religious humanism of depth psychology the end result of our overemphasis on the humanization of God. Like the scientist who studies the reaction of the eye to sunlight, we have studied the reactions of personality in its belief in God. Unlike the scientist who also studies the sun apart from its effect on the eye, we cannot, as scientists, study God as a being in himself or being itself over and apart from his influence on man. This is the realm for theology. Theology, therefore, can work together with the psychology of religion in the same manner as the scientist of the sun works together with the scientist of the eye in its relation to the sun. If we lose sight of the transcendence of God, we will ultimately lose God. The doctrines remaining to be investigated preserve this necessary tension between the transcendence and immanence of God in their influence upon the needs of personality.

While we agree with Wise that the only way any formulation of faith can vitally affect the personality is for the inner dynamics of personality to become harmonious with the ideas presented, it is precisely for this reason that the counseling relationship offers an unique opportunity for the use of such doctrines. As the four needs of people with problems are met during the course of the counseling relationship these inner dynamics undergo the change that creates the psychological moment of receptivity for profiting from these theological resources. As such the application of religious doctrine in this manner is not within the area of preaching or religious education as we usually describe these functions. The relationship between the pastor and parishioner at this "psychological moment" in the counseling relationship is unique in the functions of the ministry. The counselee is participative to the point of total response. The use of theological resources under such a circumstance is, therefore, an extension of the counseling process.

Although it may be granted that the counseling relationship is wide enough to include the application of theological resources—that the four needs of the client-centered approach need not be violated by the pastor's use of religious doctrine—it may still be questioned whether these particular resources now to be explored, though used widely and perhaps effectively in the past, are really significant to the problems of people today in view of current thought forms and especially the present emphasis in counseling. This question can only be answered by investigating these doctrines in terms of human problems and the dynamic psychology upon which the principles of counseling are based.

None of the doctrines we have discussed stand alone in the theology of the church; each is inseparable from another doctrine—that of redemption. The doctrine of man points toward redemption, the doctrine of the priesthood of the believer is the result of it, and the doctrine of Christian liberty depends upon it for the faith to face one's motives. This doctrine of redemption, the Christian means of acceptance, is known as justification by grace through faith. It is the cardinal doctrine of the Reformation. Because of this we shall refer to it in confessions representative of the three heritages of this era in the church.

From the Augsburg Confession of the Lutheran Church:

They teach that men cannot be justified in the sight of God by their own strength, merits or works, but that they are justified freely on account of Christ through faith, when they believe that they are received into grace and that their sins are remitted on account of Christ who made satisfaction for our sins on our behalf by his death. God imputes this faith for righteousness in his own sight.

From the Heidelberg Confession of the Reformed Churches:

Our Lord Jesus Christ is the mediator who is freely given unto us for complete redemption and righteousness. He is necessarily man because the justice of God requires that the same human nature which has sinned should make satisfaction for sin; but no man, being himself a sinner, could satisfy for others. He is necessarily God so that by the power of his God-head he might bear, in his manhood, the burden of God's wrath, and so obtain for and restore to us righteousness and life. We are righteous before God only by true faith in Jesus Christ; that is, although my conscience accuses me that I have grievously sinned against all the commandments of God, and have never kept any of them, and that I am still prone always to all evil, yet God, without any merit of mine, of mere grace, grants and imputes to me the perfect satisfaction, righteousness and holiness of Christ, as if I had never committed nor had any sin, and had myself accomplished all the obedience which Christ fulfilled for me, if only I accept such with a believing heart.

From the Thirty-Nine Articles of the Episcopal Church:

We are accounted righteous before God, only for the merit of our Lord and Saviour Jesus Christ by Faith and not for our own works or deservings. Wherefore, that we are justified by Faith only, is a most wholesome Doctrine, and very full of comfort.

According to these articles God justifies the sinner only on the basis of the redemptive work of Christ. Since the merits involved are not his own, his justification is by grace. The justification becomes effective in the individual when he has faith in it as his own.

OLD TESTAMENT BACKGROUND

The doctrine of justification has at least one of its roots in the Old Testament ceremonial law. In our study of the priesthood of the believer we referred to the fact that the function of the Levitical priesthood centered in the system of animal sacrifice. This system of sacrifice was an attempt to restore the communion with God disrupted by guilt. The animal's blood symbolizes the supreme sacrifice–unto death–in atonement for sin. It is an almost universal substitute for the sinner's own blood in the rituals of many ancient religions. Through this demonstration of appeasement the guilty have hoped that the deity would cease from their punishment and perhaps even restore the broken relationship.

Although animal sacrifice may be a primitive approach to the problem of guilt, the fact that it has so universally been resorted to in man's attempt to solve his basic problem would seem to indicate that it corresponds in some respect to the ultimate solution. It is this train of thought that the writer of the letter to the Hebrews follows as he interprets the animal sacrifice of Israel in terms of the redemptive work of Israel's Messiah.

> He entered once for all into the Holy Place, taking not the blood of goats and calves but his own blood, thus securing an eternal redemption. For if the sprinkling of defiled persons with the ashes of a heifer sanctifies for the purification of the flesh, how much more shall the blood of Christ, who through the eternal Spirit offered himself without blemish to God, purify your conscience from dead works to serve the living God.

This atonement through the Messiah is the "satisfaction for our sins" described in the confessions.

It is found also in the Old Testament itself. In the fifty-third chapter of Isaiah, there is the recurrent theme that the Servant of Yahweh will suffer vicariously for his people.

> He was wounded for our transgressions, he was bruised for our iniquities . . . The Lord has laid on him the iniquity of us all . . . like a lamb that is led to slaughter . . . he was cut off out of the land of the living, stricken for the transgression of my people . . . when he makes himself an offering for sin, he shall see his offspring, he shall prolong his days . . . he bore the sin of many.

Although some interpret this section to refer to Israel as a nation, it has its specific reference and theological interpretation in the redemptive sufferings of Israel's Messiah and was so identified by the New Testament writers.

GUILT AND THE ATONEMENT

While it may seem that theology traces the source of man's predicament to his sin and clinical psychology speaks only of guilt, the difference is primarily one of approach. In the doctrine of man guilt is revealed as the first of many consequences that show why rebellion (sin) is wrong. In the designation *sin,* the theology of the church gives expression to the dualistic conception of life that characterizes the biblical record. Psychology, dealing primarily with the reactions of personality, is concerned with the guilt reaction to what the individual feels is sin rather than any metaphysical analysis of good and evil. Since guilt may be both genuine and neurotic it is obvious that the nature of sin is outside the realm of psychology. The counselee who confesses to transgressions that would justify his feelings of guilt and the counselee whose anguish of guilt is obviously incommensurate with the trifles of his confession, would work havoc on any empirical classification of sins. Yet both have the same symptoms in the guilt complex and react in similar ways to the principles of counseling.

The similarity in approach by which theology deals with sin and psychology deals with guilt is further evidence that we are confronted with the same basic issue. Theology treats the problem of sin as real, and insists that it cannot be explained away or minimized if it is to be solved. Clinical psychology has discovered that the counselor cannot solve the guilt feelings of his counselee by minimizing them (simple reassurance) and even in the case of neurotic guilt, he must accept the counselee's feelings.

Guilt is fundamental to almost every problem of the human personality; it begets anxiety, is manifested in the inferiority complex and follows resentment. Any counseling—whether it is religious or secular—that is going to succeed in helping people with their problems must know what to do with the problem of guilt. The theology of the church centers around the way in which Christianity meets this very need in its doctrine of justification. So theology has something vital to say when pastoral counseling faces its fundamental challenge. The doctrine of justification meets the problem of guilt at its grass roots. If we examine guilt we see it as really a combination of two feelings: the sense of failure and the dread of just consequences. The former reveals the basic conflict between the way a person is and the way he was meant to be; it is the feeling of inadequacy or downright wickedness that results from knowing that one is not the person he should be or wants to be. The latter is really the destructive emotion of fear, but in this direct connection with guilt it can scarcely be considered apart from it from a therapeutic point of view.

The atonement of Christ also has two phases: the active obedience and the passive obedience. In the former Christ as the Second Adam redeemed the Adamic failure by overcoming the Tempter and living a life consonant with the *imago Dei.* In the latter he took upon himself the progression of sin unto death and suffered to its completion the forsakeness of the guilty. Man feels himself a failure when he does not or cannot live up to expectations—his own, other people's, and ultimately, God's. Aggravating this feeling is his sense of the futility of ever being the person he wants to be due to the inherent tendency to be selfish which he cannot always control. Theology agrees that his sense of futility is based on experiential evidence. Rather than frustrating him with demands he cannot fulfil, theology offers him a way out in the active obedience of Christ who as the Son of Man lived the perfect life for all mankind. Through the receptivity of faith the righteousness of Christ is made available to the individual sinner.

There is nothing enigmatic about man's feeling that he should be punished for his failures. Justice demands that he be punished. Obsessive and compulsive neuroses that stem from a sense of guilt are attempts to satisfy this need for punishment. But they do not work; man still has his fear—the fear that he cannot bear the punishment he deserves. Theology agrees that his fear is well founded. Since basically he feels he has disappointed God, he fears that God will forsake him. Though he may not acknowledge it, this is the unrecognized origin of his fear—theologically, this is the doctrine of hell.

In his *passive obedience* Christ suffered for mankind. In his agony in the Garden of Gethsemane and in his ordeal on the cross he paid the human debt in full. This is "the blood of Christ that purges the conscience"—the "Christ who made satisfaction for our sins on our behalf by his death"—vicariously fulfilling the demands of justice and thereby satisfying the universal desire for forgiveness and mental peace. Through the receptivity of faith the sinner is accepted and liberated.

In meeting the demands of conscience the doctrine of justification relieves the individual of the necessity for self-atonement. Many of the symptoms of neuroses and psychoses are attempts to satisfy this demand of conscience for atonement. Though the animal sacrifice was primitive it was a far more therapeutic form of atonement than our modern forms of self-atonement. There are people who because of feelings of unworthiness are subconsciously bringing on their own failures; others who are torturing themselves with anxieties and worries; others who enslave themselves to a rigid and compulsive pattern of self-denial, not for any altruistic purpose but to obtain a semblance of mental peace. In all these forms of self-atonement—often stimulated by a pusillanimous religion—there is self-inflicted suffering which becomes meritorious in balancing the budget of just deserts. They are, figuratively speaking, crosses which these individuals erect for themselves on which they can regulate their suffering to the extent that they can tolerate their right to existence. The doctrine of justification is the glad tidings to these sufferers that atonement has been made and that God accepts them as they are. When an individual is convinced that God accepts him as he is, he is encouraged to accept himself. Those whose consciences demand punishment can see that justice has been satisfied: the love of God is demonstrated in sacrifice and suffering.

AN END TO LAW

In spite of this emphasis on the satisfaction of justice from the demands of the human conscience, the Christian means of acceptance puts an end to any juridical view of the divine-human relationship. The dominant motive behind the atonement is divine love. No claim to merit or compulsion of circumstance or even ethical effects in man are responsible for its demonstration, for it is an unconditional love. It is its own stimulus. This end to the juridical demands in the divine-human relationship is interpreted in New Testament writings as the supersedure of the new covenant over the old. In the letter to the Hebrews this interpretation is symbolized in the disturbance in the elements of nature at the scene of the Sinaitic reception of the law recorded in Exodus–blazing lighting, darkness, gloom, tempest, earthquake–which struck fear into the hearts of the people. In contrast there is Jesus the Mediator of a new covenant, a kingdom that cannot be shaken. The covenant of law is designated as "on earth" while the covenant of grace is "from heaven" thus showing that the juridical demands of the human personality are both met and transcended by the concept of grace in the divine nature.

The law, in a sense, is the tyrant, along with sin, death and the devil, which is overcome by divine love. The order of retributive justice comes to its conclusion in its conflict with grace. According to St. Paul the human personality is held captive by the law. Although the law is good (spiritual) it convicts me of transgressions which I (being carnal) am unable to eradicate. That which is good in itself then becomes a curse for me from which I am redeemed by Christ who himself was made a curse for me. We die to the law through the body (death) of Christ. The atonement is redemptive love in conflict with the enemies of humanity. In this process of redemption God is not only the initiator but also the executor; in his conflict with sin, death and the curse of the law, Christ is the conqueror. His victory, therefore, is God's victory.

INCARNATION AND ATONEMENT

The concept that God in Christ redeems man is anticipated by the doctrine of the incarnation. This would answer the objection that the doctrine of justification is disturbing because, though it draws us to Christ, it alienates us from God who would demand this satisfaction in subjecting Christ to such suffering. If God was in Christ, the heavenly Parent voluntarily suffering for his children, reconciling the world unto himself, the atonement is the supreme demonstration of God's love for man. It is the perfect example of *agape*—the neighbor-centered, self-sacrificing, disinterested love that is the fulfilment of the law. This shows the inadequacy of a sole reliance upon Anselmian imagery of the atonement as a human sacrifice to God. It is not man's approach to God, but God's approach to man. One of the cloverleaf of Eastern fathers, Gregory of Nyassa, is responsible for the following concise description of the incarnation in its relationship to redemption:

> . . . that the omnipotence of the Divine nature should have had strength to descend to the humiliation of humanity, furnishes a clearer proof of that omnipotence than even the greatness and supernatural character of the miracles . . . It is the peculiar property of the essence of fire to tend upwards; no one, therefore, deems it wonderful in the case of flame to see that natural operation. But should the flame be seen to stream downwards, like heavy bodies, such a fact would be regarded as a miracle; namely, how fire still remains fire, and yet, by this change of direction in its motion, passes out of its nature by being borne downward. In like manner, it is not the vastness of the heavens, and the bright shining of its constellations, and the order of the universe, and the unbroken administration over all existence that so manifestly displays the transcendent power of the Deity, as this condescension to the weakness of our nature; the way, in fact, in which sublimity, existing in lowliness, is actually seen in lowliness, and yet descends not from its height, and in which Deity, entwined as it is with the nature of man, becomes this, and yet still is that.[1]

In this sense the incarnation is fundamental to the atonement and the atonement is fundamental to the incarnation. If the

[1] Gregory of Nyassa, "Dogmatic Treatises," etc., in *The Nicene and Post-Nicene Fathers* (New York: The Christian Literature Co., 1893), Second Series, V, chap. 24, p. 494.

"divine nature unites itself with the human nature, and be-becomes human, without ceasing to be divine," there is not only no change wrought in God's attitude toward men by the atonement, but he himself is the agent effecting the atonement. The divine nature not only substantiates the work of the human nature in the person of Christ, but uses the human nature to find the perfect expression for the divine will. This is the paradoxical nature of the atonement–God at once the Reconciler and the Reconciled–Christ reconciling us to God in his suffering and yet God himself effecting the sacrifice. From the incarnation to the resurrection there is the single and uninterrupted work of the Redeemer God.

Christ's satisfaction to the law becomes simultaneously Christ's conflict with the law and victory over it. The commemoration of the atonement in Holy Week of the church year climaxes in the Easter triumph. Based on the dualism that reckons with the reality of evil, the theology of the church centers upon the battle to victory over this evil. As such the atonement marks the divine triumph of divine love over divine wrath in the approach of God to sinful humanity and is the means through which God and the world become new in their relationship together. Atonement and salvation are for all practical purposes synonymous, and justification is simply the atonement applied at a present moment in gaining freedom from the slavery of evil. It offers forgiveness of sins through which the sinner is brought into fellowship with his Creator.

THE RESPONSE OF THE INDIVIDUAL

As an ordained minister of the church, the pastor is responsible for interpreting the theology of the church. His ministry to the guilty should not stop at saying that God forgives when there is so much more to say. It might be answered that the doctrine of justification with its basis in the atonement is primarily an intellectual concept, while guilt is a feeling, an emotional matter. But we cannot divide the personality of man into isolated parts. Personality is a unit. The intellect is a part of personality and therefore it is a part of the problem.

The confessions with their intellectual formulation are only one of several mediums of the church for the expression of its theology. The atonement is the atonement of Christ. The very name of Christ stirs the emotions of those who believe in him. A man's attachment to him in faith is as much emotion-centered as is his guilt. The response evoked is the therapeutic experience of love. The more emotional formulation of doctrine is found in the hymnody of the church which abounds in imagery of the theology of justification. Also the church's art and worship liturgy are evidences of the total response of personality to the drama of redemption. The stirring scenes in this gospel of forgiveness stimulate the powers of visualization—Christ in the wilderness overcoming temptation, his agony in Gethsemane, the scene of the crucifixion, and the excitement of the resurrection. It is significant that the re-enforcement of the doctrine of justification is the sacrament of the Lord's Supper with its dramatic memorial of the atonement and tangible reception of forgiveness. We will investigate the resources for pastoral counseling in the Lord's Supper in a later chapter.

The response from within the individual which accompanies his justification is in theological terminology, regeneration or the new birth. As justification is an act of God external to man, regeneration is an act of God within man. It is in regeneration that we witness the work of God in terms of human processes. When the sinner perceives the sacrifice of love in his justification he is moved to love in return. This is what is meant by the receptivity of faith. His attention is wrested from its fixation upon himself and his guilt and is placed upon a gracious God who has redeemed him. The experience breaks into his self-centered disposition and makes it possible for him to integrate his personality around God.

The simultaneity in occurrence between objective justification and subjective regeneration is the practical manifestation of the tension between the transcendence and the immanance of God inherent in this doctrine. This same dual emphasis is expressed in the terms *grace* and *faith*. Grace is decidedly God-centered; faith, while a product of grace, is an act of man. There is, however, a point of origin: before we have faith God has given grace.

It may be argued that justification by grace would make forgiveness so cheap that its reception would have little moment. As a result it would have little influence upon future conduct and would tend to minimize sin. This objection is actually aimed at the theology or psychology which would offer forgiveness by grace *without atonement*. Though justification is by grace its forgiveness is offered at the cost of the divine sacrifice. It is not possible that forgiveness could come easy: suffering is inevitable. The grace of God is inseparable from his suffering love. God's desire to forgive involved the necessity of overcoming the enslaving tyrants, and this led to the sufferings of Christ. When the sinner realizes how much it cost God to work out his forgiveness, he can scarcely take it lightly. Instead he is moved to a profound gratitude before such a demonstration of parental love and this becomes an incentive for obedience (sanctification).

The Christological implications in the doctrine of justification have their influence also on the response of the individual. Christ as the revelation of humanity is a stumbling block to pride. Where individuals may compare themselves with one another and often come out best, when they compare themselves with Christ the man they are humbled in the process. Since pride is the essence of sin the relationship between repentance and forgiveness is facilitated in the personal union of the divine and human natures in Christ. For the human Christ alone would lead to remorse rather than repentance. His perfection creates too great a contrast to be anything but a frustration to an aspiring humanity. In his revelation of divinity the qualities of love and forgiveness are predominant, giving hope and confidence. The two pictures together promote an optimistic humility. The godly, said Luther, trust not in their own righteousness. The experience of justification by grace humbles the recipient and at the same time inspires him. Through the experience of forgiveness there is access to newness of living.

THE DOCTRINE AND THE COUNSELING RELATIONSHIP

Although one's pride may be exposed to his consciousness in his realization of the person of Christ, its hold on him is often as much below the level of consciousness as above. In its subconscious influence pride may continue to prevent the reception of grace even though the humanity of Christ is a humbling experience consciously. Such an individual, Mr. Bush, for example, is a common experience in the counselor's office. He cannot receive because he feels he does not deserve. This close association of pride with guilt was exhibited in Adam's resistance either to repenting or to casting himself upon God's mercy. Being unable to receive grace is equivalent to being unable to receive God's atonement, which leaves the alternative of self-atonement. So Mr. Bush requires something to go wrong for him to feel relaxed. When all goes well, he becomes uneasy, for he is receiving "breaks" he does not deserve. He needs adversities such as obstacles in his path, handicaps to hold him back, reverses to hinder his progress, or having too-much-to-do to threaten his success, in order to reduce his inner conflict. Confronted with these handicaps and pressures he reaches his best efficiency in production.

Self-atonements which characterize his relationship with himself and his fellow-men extend almost automatically to his relationship to God. In fact his self-atonements to himself and to his fellow-men may be considered as being offered also to God, even though he may not consciously recognize such an oblation. The hold of unresolved guilt prevents his going the extra mile toward perfection in any area. When there is no obvious obstacle to account for this blockage, the inner conflict is heightened to an intolerable anxiety. His efforts become disintegrated and he accomplishes little. Thus if he cannot find anything to pin his anxiety on, he will soon have created a situation that will become sacrificial in nature. We have here the explanation in terms of the dynamics of personality of why God is more willing to give (grace) than we are to receive (faith). Faith is the frame of mind that can accept grace, and not, as is often suggested, an attitude that shows God my-heart's-in-the-right-place so that he cannot help but accept me. Faith is humility with hope.

Mr. Bush needs to become accustomed to accepting grace so that he can feel at home with it. But he has an emotional block which prevents this. Even though he knows the doctrine of justification by grace through faith and even subscribes to it as his creed, he is unable to live by it because there is a block between his head and his heart. The removal of this block is a task for the counseling process. As Mr. Bush talks out his feelings to his pastor he is engaging in the process that breaks down this subconscious resistance to grace. Theologically this is the process of repentance which precedes the reception of absolution. It is only as Mr. Bush unloads his guilt and anxieties and resentments that his mind will become rational enough to perceive the nature of his blockage.

In the meantime he is experiencing in the counseling relationship another influence preparing him for reception of grace. People who feel as Mr. Bush does usually were the objects of distorted love. He has been accepted conditionally and to be accepted unconditionally is foreign to his experience. Yet it is this kind of love that he receives from the pastor. In being accepted as he is in the counseling relationship, and particularly by God's minister, he is encouraged even subconsciously to think of God in terms of this same acceptance. In this manner he becomes increasingly initiated to the idea of grace, and the strangeness which heretofore repelled him is dispersed. The result of both the counseling process and the counseling relationship for Mr. Bush may be a revolution in the inner dynamics of his personality. In other words, the reception of grace brings about a rebirth.

The Christian means of acceptance is both a stimulus and a confirmation of this growth experience. The counseling process has revealed to the counselee the meaning and application of the gospel which otherwise may have been only a conventionally respected dogma without substance or root in his character make-up. As a framework for clarification it assists him to stabilize and build upon his new release. Once the dynamics of personality become receptive to grace, the application of the doctrine identifies and verifies these new insights in the light of Christian experience throughout the ages. This social support from both the church militant and the church triumphant enlarges both the scope of these opening horizons and their practical results.

The process of justification does not effect simply the removal of guilt; it also effects a reunion with the Creator, and provides power to build future living. Therapy must concern itself not only with the removal of the blockage but also with the prevention of its recurrence. The experience of justification brings about that counseling relationship with the Higher Counselor which the doctrine of the priesthood of the believer implies is the goal of pastoral counseling. The picture of God received through this acceptance is the stimulus toward this latter relationship.

FROM THE FILES OF THE CHURCH TRIUMPHANT

Before the doctrine of justification was formulated in the Confessions of the Reformation, it was experienced in the counseling process by Luther. In his earlier life he was ridden with anxiety over the state of his soul. His many efforts toward self-atonement produced only temporary respite and were followed by increased severity of anguish. Regardless of how he punished himself in monastical endeavors of fasting, exposure to the elements, and engaging in menial and beggarly tasks, he felt himself convicted by the justice and wrath of God. His agony of guilt was a problem not only to himself but to others in the monastery who feared that he was heading for a mental and physical collapse.

His counselor during this period was the vicar of the order, Johann von Staupitz, who, like any present-day counselor, wondered what grievous sin was at the bottom of the problem. From the evidence at hand, however, it appears that Luther felt guilty over his sinful condition—pride—rather than over any particular sin. From a psychologist's point of view he was probably a case of neurotic guilt. It is possible that the cold and disciplinary attitude of his parents had its influence in his anxiety over the wrath and justice of God. Staupitz would have had the sympathy of any counselor. He listened and tried to console, but to no avail. In times of exasperation he would try to snap his counselee out of his preoccupation with himself by accusing him of making a mountain out of a molehill and of prolonging his problem because he was getting a satisfaction out of it.[2]

When he saw that all of his attempts to deal with the problem through argumentation and reassurance were resisted, Staupitz tried a different approach. He put Luther to work teaching Bible. Beside being in a position where he would be helping others, he would have to deal extensively with the source book of Christianity. In studying the letters of St. Paul, particularly Galatians and Romans, in his study room in the tower of the monastery, Luther became aware for the first time of the identity of the love and justice of God in the cross of Christ and in the forgiveness offered therein by grace through faith. In this sudden and yet growing realization he found release from his anxiety over his guilt. The justice of God focusing in love is redemptive; the love of God focusing in suffering is his righteousness.

With his background in religious education Luther had undoubtedly read these passages from Paul before, perhaps several times. What was it that made the difference on this occasion? Could it not have been that Luther had experienced some growth as a result of his counseling relationship with von Staupitz and that this growth contributed to Luther's new appreciation at this particular time? If so, this is an example of the use of the Word as homework accompanying the counseling process, which we shall discuss in a later chapter. At any rate this new understanding and experience of the love of God in the redemptive work of Christ was to Luther the answer to his problem, and led to his emphasis upon the love of God in his subsequent role in the Reformation.

[2] Roland H. Bainton, *Here I Stand* (Nashville: Abingdon, 1950), p. 59.

METHOD OF USE IN COUNSELING

Using the doctrine of justification in the counseling process is not, as we have seen, a matter of simply telling the good news. The pastor's initial task is to use the principles of counseling to get to the basis of the problem. If that basis should be guilt, his next procedure is to allow this destructive emotion to spend itself through self-expression—to permit the contrition to run its course. Only after this is completed may the counselee be psychologically ready to understand the doctrine of justification and receive the absolution from God that it brings.

The many sides to the doctrine make possible a choice of approach, depending upon the situation at hand. From the beginning of the counseling relationship the pastor's attitude, if he follows the principles of counseling in spirit as well as in method, emanates the doctrine in an unspoken way in preparation for the spoken: the experience of his acceptance conditions the counselee for the grace of God after which the pastor's approach is modeled. After the destructive emotion of guilt has spent itself and the counselee becomes quieted in the course of having talked or sobbed out his problem, the pastor may use the doctrine to clarify religiously the meaning of this experience of the counselee and the insights gained in its wake. He may even use the doctrine, providing his rapport with the counselee is sufficiently strong, to stimulate these insights. There are several ways in which either may be done. The pastor may point to a picture of Christ on the wall and in his own way describe with warmth the application of his redemptive work to the problem at hand. Or, if the counselee is a regular church member, he may identify the experiences and insights at hand with certain parts of the worship service, such as the confession of sin, or with some familiar hymn stanza, or with the ceremony of the Lord's Supper, or with the meaning of pertinent festivals of the church year. He may also use Scripture directly, particularly if it has been or will be used as homework in the process of counseling, by referring to certain passages that contain elements of the doctrine and explaining them in relation to what the counselee has expressed. Another effective way of incorporating the doctrine is in connection with prayer at the close of the counseling interview in which the catharsis has taken place.

The variety both in the mental images associated with the doctrine and in the manner in which it can be brought into the counseling relationship shows that there can be no set pattern for the pastor to follow in his use of it in counseling. The individuality of each counseling relationship, the personality structure of the counselee and the pastor's own uniqueness as a person all need to be taken into account in determining the best approach in any given situation. The following interview will illustrate a case in point.

Charles Loyer, a married man with two children and a life-long church attender, is perturbed over evidences of disintegration in personality, such as tension, inability to concentrate, sleeplessness, and attacks of anxiety. The following excerpt is from the third interview in his counseling relationship with his pastor. The conversation had been centering upon Mr. Loyer's inhibiting tension.

LOYER: I get so disgusted with myself at times that I feel like throwing in the sponge.

PASTOR: You get disgusted with yourself because of this tension.

LOYER: Well, yes—and other things.

PASTOR: You feel there is something else beside this tension that is disturbing to you.

LOYER: Yeah—I suppose there is.

PASTOR: That is, you are not sure about what this something else is.

LOYER: I know what it is all right. (pause) I just don't know whether I should say anything about it.

PASTOR: You don't know whether it would be wise to tell me.

LOYER: I wouldn't know what you would think of me if I did. Every time you'd see me you would probably think of it.

PASTOR: If it would be any comfort to you, I honestly probably would not. A pastor hears quite a few things about quite a few people. I honestly don't remember them unless I make a conscious effort to do so.

LOYER: Well, even if you wouldn't, I'd think you were, and that would be the same thing.

PASTOR: I know how you feel. And you do just as you please about telling me. It may be very helpful for you to share it with me. I assure you, my only purpose is to help, not to judge. (After this several minutes passed while Loyer debated the matter with himself. The pastor alternated between rephrasing his last structuring statement and periods of *waiting* silence. It was after one of the latter that Loyer spoke.)

LOYER: It's been over with for two years now. (pause) I had an affair—a woman at the office. We started just being friends but—(pause). At first it bothered us a lot—when we had relations, that is—but after a while we didn't seem to mind, until—it got so I couldn't stand to look at myself in the mirror. I stopped it—but I can't feel forgiven. I can't because—I knew what I was doing. (He cannot accept grace because he feels he cannot accept what he does not deserve. The pastor believes it wise not to dispute Loyer's expression of hopelessness or to offer a word of forgiveness as yet. The apparent contradiction in Loyer's mind between God's unmitigated opposition to sin and his absolute forgiveness will require the dynamic of the counseling process to resolve. That one may be simultaneously justified *propter Christum* and yet remain a sinner is difficult for the guilty to perceive until they have given full expression to their guilt and grown through the counseling relationship to new levels of comprehension and insight.)

PASTOR: Because you did not do it in ignorance you feel unworthy of being forgiven.

LOYER: Yes. How could I be forgiven! Maybe it's my lack of faith. I know I can't pray right. And I'm not really straightened out either. I'm afraid of myself—I don't trust myself around other women. (So long as one feels unforgiven in his sin, he also feels helpless to overcome it. Whenever something negative seems uncontrollable, it creates anxiety. The pastor continued to reflect Loyer's feelings for the remainder of the interview. After making an appointment for the following week he suggested they close with prayer. His prayer is recorded.)

PASTOR: Dear Father in Heaven: Thou dost know how we feel in our guilt. We confess our sin and ask for thy forgiveness. Help us to receive that forgiveness. Send thy Spirit to open our hearts to the Christ who died for us. Get through in thine own way to thy servant to give him the assurance that thou didst atone for this sin also. All we need do is receive this grace. Help us, Lord, to do this. And we thank thee for thy great love that knows no limitations. In Jesus' name. Amen.

The pastor's use of prayer to bring the doctrine of justification into the counseling relationship leads to the question of the use of prayer in counseling. Is prayer for the purpose of speaking to God or for getting something across to the counselee or both? If it were only the former, the pastor could pray after the counselee had left or even silently while he was yet present. (He should do this regardless.) In speaking his prayer aloud he was not so much trying to impress the counselee as attempting to influence his frame of mind to receive God's help—to stimulate within him such a prayer, particularly since Loyer had been brought up in the atmosphere of the church and its teachings. In his subsequent returns to his pastor for counseling, Loyer began to manifest the pattern of sanctification that is described in the following chapter.

Mark Harrison entered into a counseling relationship with his pastor during a casual conversation. The following excerpt is taken from the follow-up interview.

HARRISON: I seem to lack interest in living. Perhaps it's because I have no purpose in life. I got a pessimistic view of things.

PASTOR: Life seems to lack meaning for you.

HARRISON: That's about it. It's been that way for a long time. I can remember as a kid, when somebody would die, thinking they were fortunate.

PASTOR: You felt this way even as a child.

HARRISON: Oh yeah. I guess you'd call me a defeatist. I know I spend a lot of time feeling sorry for myself. I have such an inferiority feeling whenever I'm around anybody that seems to be going places.

PASTOR: It makes you feel you are not doing as well.

HARRISON: That's the way it seems to me. But even when I do achieve something, I'm not proud about it. I don't know —I guess I feel I don't deserve it.

PASTOR: Even when you do accomplish something you don't feel you deserve any credit.

HARRISON: No—maybe it's because I never got any. My folks weren't the kind to show their feelings.

PASTOR: So you didn't know whether you were pleasing them or not.

HARRISON: No. In fact, I always had the idea that Dad was disappointed in me.

The interview continued on the nature of this father-son relationship for several minutes. We break in at the following statement by Harrison.

HARRISON: Dad was awfully dominating. It had to be his way or else. I hated it but I was afraid to go against him. Something always seemed to happen to prove he was right.

PASTOR: I suppose it seemed almost like trying to go against God.

HARRISON: In a way, yes. I guess I thought they were both ganged up against me. I think I still do. Maybe that's my trouble.

PASTOR: That God feels toward you like your father.

HARRISON: I can remember when my dog got hit by a car. I hated God for that.

And prior to the close of the interview:

HARRISON: The one thing that gave me hope came from a sermon. The preacher said how bad the church needed ministers. I thought maybe that was what I was to do, and then I'd have a purpose. But then I'd think, not me. I'm not good enough. Then everything would look hopeless again.

PASTOR: It didn't seem to you that God could take you as you are.

HARRISON: No. I guess you could say my opinion of myself isn't very high.

PASTOR: You feel God can't like you any more than you like yourself.

HARRISON: That's about it. Maybe it's all in my mind. I don't know. I get all confused.

The pastor continued in this responsive manner for the remainder of the interview. When the time came for Harrison's departure the pastor introduced the doctrine of justification by grace.

PASTOR: Mark, there is something I want you to take with you —until we meet next week. It is the meaning of Christianity. Unlike some people—even our parents—God accepts us as we are. His love for us doesn't depend on us—it depends on him. This is why we call it good news, or gospel. In Jesus Christ God breaks through our confusion to show us what he is really like. Let him take you just the way you are. He really wants to.

The pastor felt this was the time to apply the doctrine. He spoke the message in a manner that conveyed the spirit. It may be argued that Harrison would have come to this realization on his own. Yet the pastor's help at this point is in line with his position as a minister of the gospel. Harrison's problem is still a long way from solution, for the attitude of defeat is well entrenched in his personality. The realization of his acceptance by his Maker is basic to his improvement. From then on he needs to grow in this new relationship. By introducing religious doctrine into the counseling process, the pastor has prepared the way for his use of the resources for sanctification discussed in the next chapter.

SUMMARY

When the counselor reaches the bases of the varied neuroses of the human personality he usually finds the presence of guilt. As the counselor meets this fundamental problem, the theology of the church offers its fundamental doctrine as solution. The feeling of guilt may be focused upon one particular area of life and be known as the guilty conscience; it may also spread itself thinly over life as a whole and be known as the inferiority complex. Inwardly we know that we have failed to live up to expectations—our own, other people's, and ultimately God's. We also know both from internal and external witness that we live in a moral world and that there are consequences of our failures.

The doctrine of justification by grace through faith is conveyed through the atonement of Christ. In his active obedience Jesus satisfied the human need for perfection. As the Second Adam he overcame temptation and as the Son of Man fulfilled the requirements of the law. He is the Saviour from the sense of failure. In the passive obedience of Christ we see God himself sharing the sufferings of his children in order to redeem them from these sufferings. In his bitter agony and death Jesus fulfilled the universal need of man for atonement. He took upon himself the pangs of guilt and endured to their full intensities the anxieties of the forsaken. His resurrection was the triumph of God over the dark powers of the soul. He is the Saviour from the dread of consequences.

Many of the symptoms of the troubled personality are really self-inflicted punishments which result from the need for evidence by the guilty that he is suffering for his shortcomings. Even those who profess to believe in the atonement of Christ may continue to practice self-atonement to maintain their peace of mind. They have not yet been set free and are in need of counsel or they will become increasingly enslaved by this yoke of bondage. The doctrine of justification satisfies the need of the individual for acceptance (forgiveness); and for acceptance as he is (by grace); and an acceptance he may claim as his own (through faith). No pastor who has witnessed the power of this doctrine in leading another Luther out of his prison house of guilt into the free air of redemptive grace can ever doubt that it is fundamental not only to a system of theology but also to pastoral counseling.

CHAPTER TEN

The Means of Growth

The Christian means of growth is known theologically as the doctrine of sanctification and has its most systematic formulation in the Westminster Confession where it is divided into three sections. From Chapter XIII, *Of Sanctification*, we read:

> 1. They who are effectually called and regenerated, having a new heart and a new spirit created in them, are further sanctified, really and personally, through the virtue of Christ's death and resurrection, by his Word and Spirit dwelling in them; the dominion of the whole body of sin is destroyed, and the several lusts thereof are more and more weakened and mortified, and they are more and more quickened and strengthened, in all saving graces, to the practice of true holiness, without which no man shall see the Lord.
>
> 2. This sanctification is throughout in the whole man, yet imperfect in this life; there abideth still some remnants of corruption in every part, whence ariseth a continual and irreconcilable war, the flesh lusting against the spirit, and the spirit against the flesh.
>
> 3. In which war, although the remaining corruption for a time may much prevail, yet, through the continual supply of strength from the sanctifying Spirit of Christ, the regenerate part doth overcome; and so the saints grow in grace, perfecting holiness in the fear of God.

In the first section the sanctification process is defined: the sinful nature of man, forgiven through Christ, is increasingly weakened and the qualities of righteousness are gradually strengthened. In his justification the believer receives the imputed righteousness of Christ; in his sanctification he develops his own righteousness. In the second section the sanctification process is further described as an inner war between the good and evil in the believer which continues throughout his life, with the good (spirit) gaining in strength but never completely victorious over the evil (flesh). The righteousness of the believer will ultimately triumph, according to section three, because of a power outside of himself, namely, that of the Spirit of Christ. The whole process is a "growth in grace," and the end, a "perfection in holiness."

SANCTIFICATION AS PERFECTION

Christ himself gave to his church the goal of this sanctification when he said, "You, therefore, must be perfect, as your heavenly Father is perfect." "Perfect" in Greek means perfection in terms of completion–meaning full-grown, adult, mature. Our achievement of this "mature manhood," according to St. Paul, is a matter of growing up in every way "unto the measure of the stature of the fulness of Christ." He conceived of his task as a minister of Jesus Christ to "present every man mature in Christ."

The work of sanctification, or growth, is ascribed in the confessions to the Holy Spirit. In the Scriptures the marks of maturity–love, joy, peace, patience, faithfulness, self-discipline –are called the fruit of the Spirit. Our purpose is to examine how the Spirit operates to accomplish this work, particularly as it is related to the pastoral counseling process. Perhaps it is superfluous to add that in gaining such an understanding, we in no way reduce its divine character; understanding how God works glorifies rather than detracts from his role in the operation.

From the Pauline standpoint the essence of maturity is love, the binding tie of perfection. The other term for sanctification is holiness, which means purity with emphasis upon separation —from evil and unto God. Since, as we have seen, the essence of sin in biblical theology is pride, sanctification means the purging of pride from the personality by the development of its opposite pole.

The conception of Christian liberty, as we have seen, is based on love as the fulfilment or end of the law. Perfection from an ethical point of view rests upon the purity of motive in love. In the light of clinical psychology an immature person is viewed as egocentric. To achieve maturity is to break with this egocentricity by centering one's interests and energies on something outside of the self, of which the most complete and satisfying example is love. So from both the moral and psychological viewpoints love is the means to and the meaning of the Greek word for perfection.

The doctrine of sanctification begins with this love that is dynamic for maturity. It is the direct result of the justification experience. The reception of grace in divine forgiveness effects a change within personality; the experience is disruptive to old and degenerate patterns of operation and works a reorganization of interests and values which releases the creative powers of love. "We love, because he first loved us." The realization that God is not against man but against man's sin for man's sake and that he has entered the hell of its consequences to secure man's release, not only works for a solution to the problem of guilt but also organizes the personality to love in return. The internalization of the redemptive work of Christ, made possible by the penetration of this work to the depths of human suffering, stimulates a response love from the creature to this first love of the Creator. The Spirit's function in sanctification thus is based on the redemptive work of Christ and is a continuation of this work. This is in line with Jesus' own teaching concerning the Spirit: "He will take what is mine and declare it to you."[1] It is formulated succinctly in the Kansas City Confession: "We believe . . . in the Holy Spirit, who taketh of the things of Christ and revealeth them to us, renewing, comforting, and inspiring the souls of men."

The facts that sanctification is dependent upon justification for its dynamic, and that justification is dependent upon sanctification for its purpose, show the connection between these two experiences. Though sanctification is dependent upon the justification experience, the two must remain separated. To confuse in any way the sanctification process with justification would change salvation by grace into salvation by merit. The confessions are hypersensitive to any mention of merit because this would destroy the entire theological distinction of the Reformation as well as the psychological significance of Luther's experience. When a person's justification is dependent upon his sanctification it is not only justification that is jeopardized but sanctification as well. Since both the meaning of and the power for sanctification reside in the motive of love and this motive is created in the justification experience, it follows that if my sanctification is motivated also by the desire to earn or deserve, I have undercut sanctification at its incipiency because I have corrupted the love motive.

Although the experience of justification by grace is humbling, it is also enriching. The recipient has all things and his gratitude helps to make him loving and lovable. As Luther said, "Each has such abundant riches in his faith that all his other works and his whole life are a surplus with which he can by voluntary benevolence serve and do good to his neighbor."[2] Because his salvation is secure, he is released from the anxieties and defensive activities that normally tie up one's

[1] John 16:14.
[2] Martin Luther, *op. cit.*, p. 336.

psychic energies in concern for self, to devote these energies to needs beyond his own. Only as one is rich in his assurance of being loved can he be free enough to love.

The fact that this assurance is made possible through fellowship with God is one example of how the theology of the church guards against attempts to separate human activity from divine power. The abundance that precipitates love is nothing inherent in human nature, but is the result of God's activity upon human nature. The manifestation of love is nothing other than the fruit of the Spirit. The proviso of the priesthood of the believer that the resources for health and wholeness within personality stem from a reconciliation with the Creator is corroborated.

Consequently this theology produces a distinctive emphasis in the field of ethics. It is love working spontaneously, rather than obedience to laws. Nor is there any other motive than love involved such as enlightened self-interest. Even though loving brings its own reward, this also remains entirely out of the picture; even God is treated as an end in himself and not as a means to an end. Love acts regardless of how it affects the lover. It is self-sacrificial in nature because it is fashioned after the self-sacrificial love that brought it into existence. Love is outgoing; it is all-embracing. "He who loves God should love his brother also." *Agape* is always therapeutic. Because God's acceptance is fundamental to his abundance, the recipient learns to accept himself, for the love that is all-embracing includes also him.

GROWTH THROUGH RELATIONSHIP

Sanctification is a unique kind of relationship therapy. Man was created to live within a society and to establish his identity through this society; even as individuals make up society, so society makes up the individuals. In his societal framework the individual is emotionally related to certain individuals. It is these relationships that either encourage or thwart the development of personality. Even as an association tied with constructive emotions is a stimulus for confidence and progress, so the destructive ties undermine confidence by creating doubts over one's own acceptance. Although these relationships are not close in terms of security, there is a binding tie to their negative influence.

People with problems are often plagued by these ambivalent feelings in their relationships, and feel they are inwardly isolated from the company of others. Such a person has a sense of not-belonging and is tormented with the feeling of rejection and with anxiety over his insecure position. To Constance Hudson this meant that she was a failure. A religious woman in her early thirties, she considered even her need for a counselor as evidence for this failure and was ashamed that her faith was not adequate for her to handle her problems on her own. She felt that her difficulty originated in her home, since she had not received the affection she craved from her parents. Though she never felt close to anyone, she was extremely sensitive to what people thought of her. She was continually having her feelings hurt, and also in constant anxiety that she herself would hurt someone. Most people thought all she needed was a husband.

Yet her spinsterhood did not mean that romance had passed her by. In her earlier years, she had had boy friends, but each romance went by the same ill-fated route. When a young man began to show an interest in her, Constance became filled with conflicts. She was both in desperate need of this new love and yet felt unable to keep it. As a result, she was irrationally jealous of her friend and at the same time seemed to force a break-up. Her whole life had been a pattern of longing for acceptance and then preventing herself from receiving it when she had the opportunity for it. Subconsciously she felt undeserving of the acceptance she desired. Her faith was unable to solve the problem because it was fixed at an intellectual and emotional level that did not penetrate to her emotional chaos, for the same distance that existed between her and other people extended also to the person of God.

The lack of any close relationship with people affected Carlton Barnes in a different way. He could not find what he was after. Nor did he know for sure what he wanted. He strove hard for honors and when he achieved them he felt disillusioned; he sought for office and when he had it he felt empty; he was afraid of marriage because he tired too quickly of a woman once he had won her. In every new venture—and he had had plenty—his hopes were high, but in a short time he was again in the throes of discontent. Obviously his accomplishments were substitutes for something else—an effort to prove something to himself that unfortunately could not be proved in this way. He told himself he did not care what others thought and deliberately tried to give this impression, but actually he cared very much and resented this dependence. When he talked to others, he carefully concealed his own inner feelings so that they never felt they knew the real Carlton.

All his life he had felt himself different from others. Because of this he withdrew from the company of others even as a child, and thought about things that most people never bother with. When he found that because of this they did not speak his language, he felt all the more different, and alternated between feelings of inferiority and superiority toward others. He needed his accomplishments as props for his own self-acceptance because he felt that others judged him on these bases. On occasion in moments of religious contemplation, he became overwhelmed with the reality of God's presence, which gave him a temporary sense of security. Under the influence of pastoral counseling, these experiences increased and their effect became more permanent. It was the divine personality breaking through the barrier to fill the void in a lonely soul.

A satisfying relationship counteracts the destructive element of these traumatic relationships. This is the solution to man's inner division suggested by the doctrine of man. Since these relationship conflicts often begin with the parental relationship which even at its best is tainted with egocentricity, the relationship with God as parental *agape* has a particularly advantageous influence for the development of maturity. The difficulty, as witnessed in the case of Constance Hudson, is that our guilt over being a self that is generally rejected hinders our acceptance of this holy relationship. This brings us to another instance of the necessity of the justification experience as a completed act before sanctification can actually begin. Attempts to achieve this by self-atonement bring only a temporary acceptance which is broken anew by anxious doubts at each new outcropping of guilt. It is only an experience of justification by grace through faith that can sustain a relationship with the heavenly Parent in the face of repeated sin. It is this concept of justification, or parental *agape*, that is conveyed in the revelation of God in Jesus Christ, and gives to this "image of the invisible God" its dynamic for the release of the creative powers of personality that are blocked in conflict with their destructive counterparts.

GOAL FOR INTEGRATION

Before there can be freedom in personality there must be unity, for it is the inner division that produces the bondage. The process of sanctification leads to this unity. According to the doctrine, it is not only the influence from behind—prior assurance of justification—that accomplishes this integration, but the influence from the future with its goals. The issue is not only one of integration, but integration around what? Satan is integrated around a cause, and some of his earthly henchmen are not far behind.

This brings us to the goal in sanctification. Not every goal that appears to be integrating is really integrating. Take the self-center. Although it would appear to be an integration of self around self, the result is disintegrating rather than integrating, for it is the self-center that is the basis of the inner division. There is a more subtle self-center in idolatry that produces some remarkable evidence of integrating potentialities. The idol seems to redeem the individual from his egocentricity so that he gives himself wholly to it. The isms of our own era are examples of such, as their devotees in the fervor of fanaticism sacrifice themselves for their deified ideology.

The psychology of idolatry shows that the idol is actually a projection of the self-center, for the consequences of the idolatrous movement or group are associated with the destructive emotions and ultimately destroy both the idol and its adherent. Idolatry is dependent upon self-deception for its temporary guise of integration, and perpetuates rather than eliminates the inner division. This division is projected to the external world and identified as the conflict between the idol and its enemies. The idol enables the worshiper to have a center of authority outside of himself and yet to follow his own desires—to have his cake and eat it. This agrees with St. Paul's analysis of why heathen religions produce immoral living.

> Claiming to be wise, they became fools, and exchanged the glory of the immortal God for images resembling mortal man or birds or

animals or reptiles. Therefore God gave them up in the lusts of their hearts to impurity, to the dishonoring of their bodies among themselves, because they exchanged the truth about God for a lie and worshiped and served the creature rather than the Creator, who is blessed forever! Amen.[3]

Since lust is impulsive selfish desire it is disintegrating to personality, being at the pole opposite from *agape*. Idolatry is the worship of a deity created in man's image (creature).

The Christian means of growth offers as its goal in integration the God-distinct-from-self in whose image man is created. This goal is a pull upward—or rather backward, according to the doctrine of man—to man's real self. He discovers this self as he unifies his person around the One in whose image he was meant to live. Fellowship with this God-distinct-from-self is tantamount to integrating the personality in him and restores the relational characteristics of the divine image so that the individual reflects spontaneously the glory (nature) of God. He is released from the enslavement of the corruption by integrating himself around the one goal that is free from it. St. Paul describes this integration as a dying to self in order to live unto Christ.

I have been crucified with Christ; it is no longer I who live, but Christ who lives in me; and the life I now live in the flesh I live by faith in the Son of God, who loved me and gave himself for me.[4]

We find this same idea in Christ's own familiar paradox: "He who finds his life will lose it, and he who loses his life [his ego center] for my sake [the Christ center] will find it."

This integration around the revelation of the self-sacrificing God in Christ leads to the same self-sacrificing pattern in the lives of the integrated. The fruits of the Spirit—love, joy, peace, self-discipline, etc.—are not the goals of the sanctifica-

[3] Romans 1:22-25.
[4] Galatians 2:20.

tion process but by-products of the goal. The goal in sanctification is united with the love motive, which makes any sharing of the individual in the good that he does, irrelevant. The desire for sanctification (maturity, self-realization, self-improvement) would prevent sanctification if it were the goal of sanctification. Even Augustine's "highest reward" must remain the accident rather than the end of the sanctification process.

> Now this is our highest reward, that we should fully enjoy Him, and that all who enjoy Him should enjoy one another in Him.[5]

To Paul this goal is completely divorced from self-interest for it is living unto another.

> For the love of Christ controls us, because we are convinced that one has died for all; therefore all have died. And he died for all, that those who live might live no longer for themselves but for him who for their sake died and was raised.[6]

Again we note the dependence of the sanctification process upon the justification experience as the apostle identifies the death and resurrection of Christ as the stimulus that moves the individual to live for Christ. Integration in Christ is more than a living *for*, since it is an indwelling of the Spirit. The Christ center is the "Christ in you," and in the apostle's own words resembles an identity: "For me to live is Christ." [7] Yet the essential distinction between the Creator and the creature in biblical theology makes this an identity in conjunction with difference or an identity in difference.

As the goal in sanctification the Christ-centered life is the

[5] Augustine, "Christian Doctrine," in P. Schaff (ed.), *Nicene and Post-Nicene Fathers of the Christian Church* (New York: Scribners, 1917), II, p. 532.

[6] II Corinthians 5:14-15.

[7] Philippians 1:21.

"regenerated part" described in the Westminster Confession and is in "continual and irreconcilable war" with the self-centered life, even in its higher levels of enlightened self-interest. This concept of holiness is aided by the eternal nature of its goal. When an individual unifies his personality in a Christ who transcends the barrier between time and eternity, between the infinite and the finite, between life and death, his citizenship is in heaven. His perception is oriented beyond the limitations of the corruptible, and consequently beyond the disillusion and despair that lies in the wake of the disappointment and failure that is the inevitable concomitant of the influence of evil. This leads to his maturity in adjustment to the gamut of life situations.

Here is an otherworldliness that is no escape from positive and creative activity, but is rather a source of confidence for such activity—and the basis for the theology of the theological virtues. Faith when it becomes fixed on finite goals eventually becomes ineffective. Faith's anchor must rest in a world that cannot be bound by the limitations of this world if it is to be a means for accomplishment in this world. Because one's hope is in an eternal kingdom, his efforts have an eternal significance. They channel the redemptive power of God in Christ into the field of human relations. The doctrine of sanctification is in a victorious Christ—it is a *faith* in a resurrection. This is the vision of triumph that inspires the love that hopeth all things.

With these resources for holiness, pastoral counseling has an advantage over its secular counterparts in achieving fulness of living. The end is no withdrawal to safer ground, but a thorough wholeness of personality that can dare the devil and overcome limitations. We turn now to the relation of this doctrine to the counseling process.

SANCTIFICATION IN COUNSELING

As the counselee finds he can express himself with satisfaction to his pastor, he should find it easier to exercise such expression to God. This is especially true if the pastor can tie down the correlation by giving him a few practical pointers on how to realize this relationship with God–such as: "You can talk to God just as you talk to me. Tell him whatever is on your heart–even as you give expression to your feelings in here. God accepts you just as I do." This can be done at the close of the session in connection with the suggestions for homework which we shall discuss in the next chapter.

God is far more necessary to the needs of personality than is usually allowed by authorities in the field of psychotherapy. For this reason, the pastoral counseling program may enter depths often avoided by secular counselors and mental health clinics. There is a religious tension–a need for a meaning and purpose of life–which is actually a need for God. "In him all things hold together." It can readily turn into an inner anxiety when it is unallayed either by rationalization or by God-substitutes. This religious tension comes in part from the disturbance of conscience described in the confession. If the "irreconcilable war between the spirit and the flesh" has no resolution it leads to the feeling of despair described in the seventh chapter of Romans.

> I do not understand my own actions. For I do not do what I want, but I do the very thing I hate. Now if I do what I do not want, I agree that the law is good. So then it is no longer I that do it, but sin which dwells in me . . . Wretched man that I am! Who will deliver me from this body of death?

It is the religious answer of the Christian gospel that St. Paul gives to this rhetorical question: "Thanks be to God through Jesus Christ our Lord!" This means that the conflict is overcome by being able to face it with the pressure of guilt (feeling of condemnation) removed.

Although it is understandable that secular psychotherapists would feel inadequate in theological matters, this does not justify the procedure of some to set aside the theological problems of their patients as symptomatic rather than basic to their difficulty. While this may be true some of the time, it is not true all the time; one's relationship to his God may be fundamental to his problem and not merely a surface issue.

Mrs. Anderson was satisfied with and benefited by psychiatric help, but she felt she wanted also to see a pastor. She stated the reason for this at the beginning of her first appointment.

MRS. ANDERSON: I wanted to see you because I feel there is a religious problem at the bottom of my trouble.

Later:

MRS. ANDERSON: I label myself an atheist, and I really think I am one, but—(pause).

PASTOR: It doesn't settle the problem, is that what you mean?

MRS. ANDERSON: Well it does until—until I wonder if I am wrong.

PASTOR: And this is disturbing?

MRS. ANDERSON: Yes, it is.

PASTOR: In other words atheism gives you more peace than believing there is a God.

MRS. ANDERSON: Definitely. Everything's going round and round inside of me right now—just talking about it.

It is obvious that Mrs. Anderson's thought—and therefore mental picture—of God is charged with destructive emotions, and that her atheism is her refuge from this pursuing image.

The counseling that helps her meet her basic problem must ultimately reach the anxiety associated with her relationship with God. Here is the specific need for pastoral counseling.

Since growth in self-understanding is the prerequisite for growth in overcoming and since "the remnants of corruption abideth still in every part and for a time may much prevail," it is apparent that the counselee's growth is characterized by an increasing awareness of the extension of his corruption. In this sense the process of sanctification intensifies the conflict between the spirit and the flesh. All growth is structured by the realization of *simul justus et peccator* (justified and yet a sinner), for this honest appraisal of himself enlarges God's grace for the believer, and in so doing expands his faith. God works through the imputed righteousness by faith to develop righteousness of character within the believer—by his grace through the believer's faith.[8]

The believer's fellowship with God that results from the experience of forgiveness is continually threatened by these growing insights which precipitate again the despair of overcoming the barrier of guilt. Sanctification is a continuous struggle against this disruptive concomitant of its own process. Yet it need not threaten the fellowship, for it is justification and not sanctification that is the basis for the fellowship. The "through Jesus Christ our Lord" triumph over the defeatism of the seventh chapter of Romans is amplified in chapter eight to include the uninterruption of the divine-human relationship.

For I am sure that neither death, nor life, nor angels, nor principalities, nor things present, nor things to come, nor powers, nor height, nor depth, nor anything else in all creation will be able to separate us from the love of God in Christ Jesus our Lord.

What happens to prevent this expected interruption is de-

[8] Albert C. Outler, *Psychotherapy and the Christian Message* (New York: Harper, 1954), pp. 183-184.

scribed by the death and resurrection analogy of St. Paul and later of Luther. As Christ died on the cross to accomplish the redemption from sin, so the believer's old Adam is crucified with Christ, and as Christ rose from the dead in triumph over the forces of evil, so the believer rises from the death of his old nature to new life in the Second Adam. Both the Apostle and Luther see in baptism the sacramental demonstration of this identification with the redemptive work of Christ. To the apostle this inner renewal is a circumcision of the spirit which he associates with the reception of the new covenant rite of baptism.

> In him also you were circumcised with a circumcision made without hands, by putting off the body of flesh in the circumcision of Christ; and you were buried with him in baptism, in which you were also raised with him through faith in the working of God, who raised him from the dead.[9]

To the Reformer the baptismal covenant is renewed daily as the believer relives the death and resurrection sequence. In answer to his catechetical question, "What does such baptizing with water signify?" Luther says:

> It signifies that the old Adam in us, together with all sins and evil lusts, should be drowned by daily sorrow and repentance, and be put to death; and that the new man should daily come forth and rise, to live before God in righteousness and holiness forever.

The process of repentance which Luther describes as a drowning of the remaining corruption expands the scope of the believer's vision. Old mental pictures are rejected for new and enlarging ones and the crooked places are made straight. Accompanying this change is a sorrow over the error of former perceptions and the depressing vision of expanding self-knowledge. Yet the sorrow of repentance is not destructive to personality as is despair, but rather constructive

[9] Colossians 2:11-12.

because it is sorrow with hope. Sanctification is a *becoming* process. Not as though the believer had already attained, but rather reaches forward to those things which are ahead. The hope consists of turning one's attention from the things which are behind in order to press toward the goal of maturity in Christ Jesus. This is possible because each new perception into our corruption that takes place in the process of repentance creates the guilt that turns the believer again to the source of his forgiveness. Each new experience of forgiveness increases the believer's appreciation of the *agape* centered in the cross. The emotion of gratitude intensifies the divine-human relationship and becomes the means for renewed confidence in the power of God. It is in this manner that the experience of repentance results in the drowning of the old man and the coming forth of the new, as the process of sanctification is anchored in the assurance of the baptismal covenant that the "regenerate part doth overcome."

There is a subtle temptation—a particular danger in counseling—for an individual to become egocentric in his endeavors toward growth. Having experienced a certain amount of progress, he may become enthusiastic in his efforts to gain more. Unknowingly he may assume an activist role that is doomed to defeat. He falls into the error of "trying too hard" and becomes tense in his efforts to overcome irritation, moods, and among other things, tension. Finally, he may break down in complete frustration. What has happened is that self-improvement has become its own motive under the disguise of religious endeavor and, as always in religious pursuits, when one actively seeks the reward, he disqualifies himself. Sanctification is also by grace through faith. Here is where the passive orientation of the mystics has a point. Although they often fail to keep the distinctive Christian emphasis upon the differentness between the Creator and the creature, their endeavors to step aside and allow God to take over are sound in the pursuit of sanctification. It is the Holy Spirit himself that is to be sought, rather than his fruits. Growth is growth in grace. It is an awareness of God behind the entire process, working within and without, and faith that he will move us to will and to do of his good pleasure. Popularly speaking, it is the art of "letting go and letting God." The believer's co-operation is directed by the mental image of the predominance of God.

Harry Donaldson had been counseling with his pastor concerning his nervous tension. He became quite encouraged with his progress and confident of his ability to continue it. About a month after he had discontinued his appointments with his pastor, he began to notice that he was slipping. At first it did not concern him greatly because he felt that he could easily restore his tranquility by concentrating more fully on the ways that he had found successful before in combating tension. But this time they did not seem to have their old power. Harry grew concerned and tried all the harder, but the more he tried the more tense he became. He was reluctant to return to his pastor because he had sounded so sure that he had his problem licked. When he did return, it was not to secure more help, but to tell his pastor of the experience that had redeemed him this second time. The following is an excerpt from Harry's story:

> Even my devotional life—which I counted on to bring me back to where I was—seemed to fail me. The more I tried to contact God the more panicky I became. All I could think about was that I was back in the old rut. Finally I just couldn't fight any longer. I said, "God, I'm beat. If this is the way you want me, all right." Then it seemed a peace came over me. It's hard to describe it. It was as though God was right there and everything was all right. I guess maybe that was what was the matter—I had thought it all depended on me—and what I did.

The concept of providence is inseparable from sanctification. When an individual believes in the Power working behind the scenes, he finds a certain stabilization that tends to keep him out of his own line of vision so that his line of direction is focused on the bigness of God. The realization of providence is the needed therapy for the external tensions that are part of the warp and woof of life and that are a continual factor in bringing pastor and parishioner together. Probably because they appear wholly or in part beyond the accountability of the counselee, these troubles and sorrows create an acute religious anxiety. His outlook on affairs is temporarily shaken and he needs a renewed insight into the doctrine that God uses and overrules evil for the ultimate good. The Christian interpretation of suffering as chastening has helped myriads of sufferers to accept their lot in a positive and triumphant manner.

> Now no chastening for the present seemeth to be joyous but grievous; nevertheless afterward it yieldeth the peaceable fruit of righteousness unto them which are exercised thereby. Wherefore lift up the hands which hang down, and the feeble knees; and make straight paths for your feet . . .[10]

Here is no stoical acceptance of tragedy but an integrative concurrence in a providence whose trustworthiness becomes a sufficient answer to the protests inherent in suffering. It is the sort of maturity in his counselees that the pastor would hope to achieve in his counseling.

This procedure for dealing with the remnants of the corruption, both within and without, belongs in pastoral counseling. While it is usually the better procedure to allow the counselee to develop his own insights into these patterns of sanctification, the pastor's ability to relate the heritage of the covenant to these growing insights will do much to deepen

[10] Hebrews 12:11.

their meaning for the counselee. The pastor's own experience in the area of sanctification is invaluable in this respect. The great spiritual counselors of the ages have been men who knew the ways of God with man from personal fellowship—men like Brother Lawrence, Gerhard Groote, John Frederic Oberlin, who, while we may criticize some of their counseling procedures and their mystical emphases, nevertheless have shown from their labors that the relationship of master to disciple belongs in the area of pastoral counseling. As the counselee is helped to discover these trodden paths toward sanctification, he will understand the processes of soul that the confessions of the church attempt to formulate as they describe how the regenerate part overcomes. The doctrinal framework of the means of growth will become for him a valuable reference of the intellect upon which to place his developing insights so that the resultant clarity of pattern will become a stimulus for further insights into the perfecting of holiness.

John Marshall was hypersensitive to what others thought of him, and withdrew in defeat at any evidence that his rating was below what he desired. Because he had been to other sources for counseling, he frankly told the pastor that the insights revealed in their relationship were things he knew beforehand. But still there was no growth. He was frustrated over himself and most of his time was spent in feeling miserable about it. He wanted to believe in Christianity, he said, but he was afraid he would believe it because he wanted to, rather than because it was true. It was this statement that led the pastor at the close of the interview to describe the use of selected Bible passages—discussed in the next chapter—as a help to faith. Marshall looked rather skeptical and said he had tried such things before and they had not worked. He took the list of passages even though the pastor told him not to use them until he felt it would do some good.

To the pastor's surprise Marshall returned the following week saying the passages had helped and that he felt much better. He seemed to want to talk about the workings of personal religion. The following is a sample.

MARSHALL: I'm wondering if a person's prayers aren't answered sometimes because he doesn't really believe that his answers can happen.

PASTOR: You believe that God needs a receptive mind on our part to give us what we pray for.

The next interview revealed a temporary recession.

MARSHALL: I felt good for several days. But I had a feeling it couldn't last and the harder I fought it, the more it got me.

PASTOR: You felt it was too good to last.

MARSHALL: Yes—and it seemed that part of me was bringing up things to worry about and another part was fighting against thinking about these things. (His attitude toward himself cannot tolerate his happiness, and his regression or mood is caused by a recurrence to his mind of some phase of himself as a failure.)

PASTOR: It's a fight against yourself, isn't it? And it seemed that you were doomed to lose it.

MARSHALL: Then when I realize I am right back where I started from—I get a terrible feeling of discouragement—that I'm licked—that it's too late. I get mad at God for allowing it.

PASTOR: It seems at these times that God isn't helping you like he should.

MARSHALL: That's the way it seems. I get disgusted with prayer and everything. I suppose it's really that I'm mad at myself.

PASTOR: When you are mad at yourself, or dislike yourself, it is hard not to dislike others—even God.

MARSHALL: And I think you dislike yourself even more because of the things you think about others. And about God too.

PASTOR: It's a vicious cycle downward, isn't it?

MARSHALL: Maybe I'm trying too hard . . .

And later at the close of the interview:

PASTOR: You can expect these dips, John, for they are part of the growth pattern. The thing that saves us is that God can love us even in these dips, and if we trust him, he will bring us out of them in better shape than before. This is the meaning of that verse you have—"Acknowledge him in all thy ways."

The following interview found Marshall feeling much better again.

MARSHALL: I think we're getting someplace. This business of not liking myself—I think that's the trouble, really.

PASTOR: I see.

MARSHALL: I think I've been trying to do it all myself. Before when I prayed I think I was *using* God. Now—it's hard to explain it—but I think God intends to give me himself.

PASTOR: He is becoming more important to you in himself.

MARSHALL: I never realized Christianity was like this—what it can mean.

It is this experience of the God of love in our needs that enables us to talk the language of the saints which the "natural man perceiveth not."

As a minister of the church the pastor has at his disposal to supplement his counseling the unique resources for social therapy which this institution provides. As the communion of saints, the church is a fellowship that envelops the individual in a group solidarity that opposes any tendency to egocentric isolation. St. Paul's statement that we should not lie one to another because we are all members one of another, illustrates how the individuals within the church fellowship are united with each other, even as the members of the human body join with each other in their functioning together under the direction of the head, which in the case of the church is Christ. This is the sort of social identification in which people with problems are often lacking and which is needed for their recovery. The church is far more than a social fellowship. The members are related to God before they are related to each other, and are related to each other because they are related to God. The divine-human relationship within the church preserves the individual in his group association. He can give himself to the church as a member to its body, without curtailing his development as an individual in personal fellowship with his Creator. The church is also a fellowship united by a commission; it offers not only a sense of belonging but a sense of urgency. The counselee finds purpose for himself in the need for workers within the kingdom of Christ to extend this kingdom through the fellowship created by his Spirit.

As the body of Christ, the church fellowship is an extension of his redemptive love. Since growth in holiness is equivalent to growth in the capacity for love, the church fellowship offers a concrete opportunity for the reception and practice of this love. Although some people may use the church as an escape from their problems, those who are counseling with their pastor would be facing these problems. The self-understanding that grows out of the counseling relationship would expose whatever subconscious tendencies one would have to busy himself with the externalities of religion in order to side-step the internalities. The end for which pastoral counseling is the means—communion with the Head—is supported by the activity of corporate worship. The sermon as a discourse on the life of the spirit may both emphasize the insights achieved in the counseling relationship and stimulate additional ones. As a prophetic challenge, it may inspire the counselee to self-giving activity that accelerates growth. The holiness of the church centers in its power to produce holiness in the lives of its people. At work within the social therapy of group worship are the resources of Scripture and sacrament for the sanctification of the participants. We turn now to these powers committed unto the church as they are described in the theological doctrine of the means of grace.

SUMMARY

The more one is able to love, the more he develops the qualities of integration and adjustment to reality that mark the mature person. From both the ethical and the psychological points of view, love is the way to perfection, both in purity and in maturity. If our sanctification is allowed to become confused with our justification, then our motive for pleasing God is no longer one of love and gratitude, but one of earning and deserving. Hence we have the entrance of a self-interest motive into our living which is a deterrent rather than an incentive to growth. Justification must come first and be a completed experience, since the sanctification process is dependent upon the mind-set which results from it. Each time the sinner is drawn to the cross in new repentance, he gains a deeper appreciation of the gift of forgiveness. This ever-increasing gratitude for the righteousness which is imputed unto him becomes the motive in his own righteousness. Because he knows that he is accepted of God by grace, his tension is released and he is free to love. When the barrier of guilt is removed through the justification experience, he is brought into an interpersonal relationship with God which gives him security and inspires him with confidence even more than would a human relationship. Whenever the feeling of guilt returns, the separation from God also returns. Again it is evident that the justification experience must precede that of sanctification to make either of them possible.

According to the psychology of personality an individual needs a goal around which to integrate his life if he is to mature. The doctrine of sanctification has its goal for living in God himself—one that is worthy of the complete devotion of a human life and able also to hold this devotion for a lifetime. The goal of pastoral counseling is to present every counselee mature in Christ Jesus—that he may live not unto himself but unto Christ. When one reaches even the initial stages of Christ-centered living, his personality is well on its way toward becoming complete and made whole.

CHAPTER ELEVEN

The Means of Grace

1. THE SCRIPTURE IN COUNSELING

The church as an institution has been entrusted with means through which the Spirit of God offers his grace to the believer. These means of grace are the Word of God and the sacraments. They are not to be thought of as something between God and man but rather as ways in which God is received. Although means of grace signifies ways of receiving God's gifts, no gift of God is separable from God himself.

As we discuss the application of the Word and the sacraments to the counseling process, it may seem that we are going beyond the counseling process into religious exercises. From the secular standpoint we are. Pastoral counseling, however, is counseling within the framework of the church. To separate the church's means of grace from pastoral counseling would divorce pastoral counseling from its Christian context. Even from a secular point of view the counseling experience extends beyond the counseling office. The experiences of the counselee outside of the actual counseling period implement the progress of the counseling. Despite their apparent helpfulness or hindrance they are the raw material for the stimulation of insights.

The doctrine of the means of grace describes the role which

the Word and sacraments occupy in the Christian faith. Calvin states in his *Institutes:*

> Let us abide by this conclusion, that the office of the sacraments is precisely the same as that of the word of God; which is to offer and present Christ to us, and in him the treasures of his heavenly grace.

To this the Augsburg Confession agrees: "Through the Word and Sacraments as through instruments, the Holy Ghost is given, who worketh faith where and when it pleaseth God in them that hear the Gospel."

The Word is the gospel, the message of redemption, the revelation of justification by faith, the proclamation of God's unconditional love. It is God speaking to man—to the individual. Its purpose is to effect a response in man. The power of the Word is the testimony of the Holy Spirit that convinces the recipient to submit to his claims. Although the Word, as it is associated with the Scriptures, and the sacrament have been generally recognized as resources for the pastoral ministry to the troubled, they are also recognized by the more discerning as an escape from responsibility for the pastor and means of avoiding God for the parishioner. Our purpose is to go beyond Scripture and sacrament to the theology of the church concerning Scripture and sacrament in search of an effective procedure for the use of these means of grace in pastoral counseling. In this penetration into the historic wisdom of the church we shall concern ourselves first with the doctrine of Scripture.

THE SCRIPTURE AS REVELATION

When we speak of the Word we are dealing with the concept of revelation. For Christian theology revelation is climaxed in Jesus Christ. The *Logos* which was from all eternity was made flesh in the personal appearance in history of Jesus of Nazareth. This tremendous breakthrough of God into the course of humanity is the basis for the *Deus dixit* of the Word. Contact with the Word brings one in contact with this event, or as Calvin said, in the Word Christ is presented to us.

Since the Word is incarnate in Christ it is recorded in literary form in the Scripture. This is obvious since it is the Bible that preserves for us what we know about Jesus. The Bible is the Word of God because Jesus as the Christ is its central content. It is the living Word of God because God continues to speak in Christ. It is a means of grace because the Holy Spirit who is the Spirit of Christ functions through the *Logos* to redeem. The division of the Scripture in Old and New Testaments fails to disrupt its unity if the Old Testament is understood in terms of the revelation of God in Christ. Through the Word, lived in a Person, received by the church, preserved in recorded symbols, proclaimed in the office of the ministry, alive in Christian conversation, God is revealed to man. In our study of the preceding doctrines we have discussed the use in counseling of the Word as God's message to man. We are now specifically concerned with the use of the Scripture as the record of this Word.

Often people have a warped perception of the Bible so that even the mention of it in the counseling process may hinder their free expression. To them it represents an authority they both fear and resent. They think of it in the penal terms of the letter of the law and as always the letter kills. Thinking of the Scriptures as a means for the reception of the Spirit counteracts this static conception of the Word. Through this sword of the Spirit which is sharper than any two-edged sword, the individual is pierced to the dividing asunder of his soul and spirit, of his joints and marrow, to the discernment of the thoughts and intents of his heart. The revelation of God is not completed in the Bible until the Holy Spirit has extended this revelation to the spirit of the individual. In this manner he has his own experience of Jesus as the Christ and adds his own witness to the Word. The spoken Word continues even though the Word is written, and is indebted to the written Word for its perpetuity. This strictly functional conception of the Scriptures has as its ultimate end the reorganization of the values and interests of the one who exposes himself to the Word.

This reorganization of personality is not the result of a mere intellectual perception of the written symbols. To function as a means of grace the Scripture would have to do more than present doctrines to the reason of man. As Calvin says:

> ". . . the testimony of the Spirit is superior to all reason. For as God alone is sufficient witness of himself in his own word, so also the word will never gain credit in the hearts of men, till it be confirmed by the internal testimony of the Spirit. It is necessary, therefore, that the same Spirit, who spake by the mouths of the prophets, should penetrate into our hearts . . ." [1]

For the Spirit to accomplish his work, he must make his testimony creditable to the hearts of men as well as their heads. The Word as God's self-revelation is the disclosure of his self-giving. The power of this disclosure reduces the conflict of loyalties within the believer. Through the work of the Spirit the revelation of Christ as Saviour becomes an event in human experience and the response is a spontaneous acclaim of Christ as Lord. The Word is a message from God that subdues the recipient. When, therefore, the Bible functions as a means of grace God is revealing himself to man and is acting upon man to make of this revelation the center of his living.

[1] John Calvin, *Institutes* (Philadelphia: Westminster), vol. I, bk. 1, chap. 7, p. 90.

USE IN COUNSELING

This doctrinal development of the Scripture as a means of grace suggests a way in which Scripture may be used in pastoral counseling. The incarnation of the Word in Christ is both a finished work and an ongoing process. Its purpose is to unite the human with the divine in the individual personality. This union is a dynamic rather than a static condition and requires the continuous reception of the testimony of the Spirit to maintain and expand its realization. As a means through which the Holy Spirit works to release the creative powers of personality, the Bible can serve as the needed inspirational support for the counseling process, which can empower the insights gained through counseling with faith in God and zeal for his kingdom.

In the Augsburg Confession the teaching concerning the means of grace is incorporated in the article concerning the office instituted to administer these means. Trained by education and experience as a scientist of the Word, the pastor is the "workman who has no need to be ashamed, rightly handling the word of truth." This knowledge and skill, obviously a necessity for the preaching and teaching of the Word, is needed also in the counseling ministry. The pastor knows the counselee and his problem and he knows the Scriptures; he ought, therefore, to be able to join the Scriptures with the counselee at the proper spot. If the counselee is receptive to the Scriptures, the pastor can be his helper to receive from it the grace he needs.

The use of the Bible as a means of grace should not be understood as a mechanical process. The doctrine of the Word as well as the sacrament dare have no *ex opera operatum* interpretation. This was made clear in the article in the Augsburg Confession: "For through the Word and Sacraments as through instruments, the Holy Ghost is given, who worketh faith *where and when it pleaseth God* in them that hear the Gospel." (Italics my own.) Man does not use the means of grace to control God; rather God uses them to communicate with man. God is the free agent who by his own decision has chosen to make the Bible revelation. In our use of the Bible we put ourselves in position to be influenced by his Spirit through the means he has chosen to reveal himself—that is, as much as we are capable of comprehending through the work of this same Spirit. Although the means of grace are used by God to communicate with the individual, they are not something between God and the individual. The event that unifies the personality is the God-with-us encounter and the manner in which this is effected is bound up in the mystery of the relationship between the Spirit "who worketh faith when and where it pleaseth God" and the human will.[2] Yet even our faith is preceded by his grace; and in our obedience the accent remains upon his initiation.

Using the Bible in pastoral counseling according to the method suggested by the doctrine of the means of grace fits into the description of homework for counselees described by Carl Rogers. "Some counselors," says Rogers, "give their clients 'homework' of some variety between contacts, topics they are to think about, aspects of their situations which they are to observe." [3] By giving his counselee pertinent selections of Scripture to think about for homework the pastor is attempting to facilitate the procedure by which God has chosen to work his healing power. The use of the Bible as homework in the counseling relationship should not be construed as something apart from the counseling process. The Holy Spirit uses

[2] A careful analysis of this mystery is contained in *The Revelation and the Mystery of Grace*, a pamphlet by Conrad Bergendoff, Augustana College, Rock Island, Ill.

[3] Carl R. Rogers, *Counseling and Psychotherapy* (Boston: Houghton Mifflin, 1942), p. 166.

this interpersonal relationship to effect the apperception of the message of the Word to the individual. In the sensitive condition of soul which usually characterizes people with problems, the counseling process may be the contributing factor in the transfer of the Word from the head to the heart. Because of its characteristic moments of insight this relationship is one of the most receptive situations for the appropriate use of scriptural therapy. Since both counseling and the use of Scripture are in themselves growth stimulants, they work reciprocally for the greater efficacy of each and, consequently, for the more rapid and thorough progress of the counselee. This incorporates the counseling process in the circuit in which the Spirit works when and where it pleases God, and reveals the relationship of the office of the ministry to the means of grace as it is described in the Augsburg Confession article: "That we may obtain this faith, the office of teaching the Gospel and administering the Sacraments was instituted."

For the pastor simply to tell his counselee to read his Bible as homework would probably only frustrate him more than he already is. Most people, including church members, are unable to read the Bible discriminately and are even more unable to use it as a means of grace. Not all parts of the Bible are of equal value for help in the disturbances of personality. This is doubly true for people with problems, who, because of their unresolved guilt feelings, may have a warped perception of passages emphasizing condemnation. Neurotic fears over the sin against the Holy Ghost are an extreme example of this. Theologically the Word is divided into two parts, the law and the gospel. Naturally it is the gospel that is most helpful in counseling. Some have even questioned whether the law can be a means of grace; rather they feel it prepares the spirit for the reception of grace through the gospel. However, when the law is received in the spirit of the gospel (acceptance) it can be an effective means of grace, and when used discriminately can be of great help in overcoming certain besetting character handicaps. The law of God without the grace (gospel) of God is a curse rather than a blessing, but with the grace of God it becomes transformed into an angel of light.

During the course of my counseling ministry I have gathered a group of passages that I have found particularly helpful when used as means of grace to support the counseling process. I have listed them in a classification which is both arbitrary and overlapping, but which is still a handy reference from which to choose the verses needed at the moment. Although these verses are only a scattering of the total Scriptures they are pithy digests of the divine message of justification and its results. As such they reveal from the various angles of human need the meaning of Christ as Saviour.

Faith and Confidence
Habakkuk 3:17-18.
Psalm 31:24.
Matthew 5:6.
John 15:7.
II Corinthians 5:7.
II Corinthians 9:8.
Philippians 4:13.
Colossians 3:23.
Hebrews 11:1.

Comfort and Security
Isaiah 26:3.
Isaiah 41:13.
John 14:1.
I Corinthians 10:13.

Hope in Despair
Psalm 42:5.
Jeremiah 29:13.
Romans 8:28.
Hebrews 12:11-12.
I Peter 5:7.

Overcoming Anxiety and Resentment
Philippians 4:6-7.
II Timothy 1:7.
Hebrews 13:6.
I John 4:18-19.

Overcoming Guilt
Isaiah 43:25.
Romans 5:1.
I John 1:9.

Guidance
Isaiah 30:21.
Proverbs 3:5-6.

Self-discipline
Psalm 141:3.
Proverbs 16:32.
II Corinthians 10:5.
Philippians 4:8-9.
James 1:19-20.

The Christ Center
Matthew 6:33.
Matthew 16:25.
Galatians 2:20.
Galatians 5:24.
I Corinthians 13:4-5.

Some may prefer longer sections of Scripture as homework to counseling. Some types of minds are particularly receptive to the rational appeal of the Book of Proverbs. Others are open to the depth of feeling in the Psalms and in certain chapters of Isaiah. The parables of Jesus appeal to the imaginative. The upper room discourses from the Gospel of John are helpful to those longing for the experience of reunion and acceptance. Certain chapters from the Pauline and general epistles appeal to the searching mind. I prefer the shorter selections because they allow for more variety in the homework. Also shorter passages lend themselves better to concentration and to memorization. Although the pastor may have a collected list of such passages, it adds to the personal touch if he makes out a special list at each occasion. I usually list only the references and choose from the list those most pertinent to the case at hand.

Knowing when to use the Scriptures as homework is almost as important as knowing how to use it. I have been told of a certain physician who is known as Dr. Pink Pill by his community because he regularly hands out pink pills to his patients. These pills may be very good pills and probably are even different kinds of pills, but to the people the same color and shape makes them the same pill. Because the physician appears to hand out these pills indiscriminately to his patients, his remedy has become the butt of humor and as a result his prestige has suffered. The pastor's use of the Scripture as homework should not degenerate into the traditional pink pill. Nor should he use it as an escape from his own feelings of inadequacy in a counseling situation. As homework the Scripture is to supplement the counseling process and not to substitute for it.

When to use the Scriptures in counseling depends as much upon the counselee as upon the nature of his problem. Although as we have noted the problem is inseparable from the person who has it, except the person is receptive to such homework, the assignment of it may do more harm than good.

There are people even in our churches who experience a negative reaction at the mention of the Bible. If they thought the pastor would try to get them to read the Bible as a way of helping them, they probably would not go to him with their problems. They want to be free from any preaching—from any coercion toward a religious solution, and yet they subconsciously may realize that religion holds their answer. They might be receptive to the Word if it were dissociated from their distorted mental pictures of the Bible, the church and religion. As one man told me when I precociously mentioned the Bible homework plan as a means of breaking into his spirit of hopelessness and defeat: "I don't think it would do any good. That's all I've heard since I've been a kid is read your Bible. I'd read the verses—but it wouldn't mean anything to me. It would just be reading words."

Others are more or less apathetic about religion. They do not particularly see where it applies to their problem. Unless their situation becomes so desperate that they are willing to try anything, they may take only a perfunctory interest in such a plan. They are like the people who go to Dr. Pink Pill and tolerantly accept his medicine, but forget to take it. In these instances the pastor is wiser to confine his use of the Word to the spirit of his pastoral relationship where it will not be resisted because of its ostensibly religious earmarks. In this manner he manifests the Word through his person (becomes a little Christ to his neighbor), and in time may discover that the earlier barriers to the written Word have been dissolved by this relationship.

There are those also who realize that religion may have a meaning for their problem and are interested enough in their problem and in religion to invest some time in this homework. They may have been in this receptive frame of mind at the first interview or may have become this way in the course of the counseling relationship. When the pastor perceives that the suggestion for the homework is advisable he can explain at the close of the interview the nature of the plan and ask the counselee if he would be interested in some selected verses for this purpose. If there is a lack of response he may suggest they not try it as yet. If his experience is anything like mine he will find most of those he asks quite appreciative. People who are troubled are often eager for something such as this to minister to their spiritual life where they feel a need for strength. They also want some help in using the Bible in a devotional way. After they have used the verses they are often surprised and delighted to discover that the Bible contains such helpful material. Even after their problem has eased some will continue with their homework because they have found in it a satisfying devotional practice. In fact this use of Bible verses is to acquaint the counselee with the message of the Bible so that he may be encouraged to explore further and receive more. It is an introduction to the use of the Bible as the Word of God.

It is helpful to explain the plan in terms of its doctrinal basis. The purpose of Christian theology is to prepare the mind for the reception of Christ. There is nothing automatic in the transition between reading the Bible and receiving the Word. The reception of grace is received by faith. While faith is a product of grace it is not by this fact outside the realm of human freedom. It is a personal attitude which can be encouraged by the pastor's briefing concerning the theological dynamics behind the homework. After the counselee has shown an interest the pastor may say something to this effect: "We say the Bible is God's Word. This means that God speaks through it to us. Therefore it is our part to do a good job of listening. After you look up a passage hold your mind on it for about a minute or two. Just think about what it says. Then take the next one and do the same. Continue this until you have put in about twenty minutes. If you can do it in the morning it will give you a good start for the day. In this list I am giving you, some passages will mean more to you than others. Use these more. It will help even to memorize them so that you will have them with you whenever you need to recall them."

By giving him a generous selection of verses we are allowing for the fact that what goes on sometimes between the Spirit and the individual is unpredictable. It may not be the pastor's favorite selection that gives grace to the counselee but rather one of his lesser favorites. There was the counselee, for example, who told me how much one of the verses from Isaiah that I had given him had meant to him. I asked him which verse it was and from his description I did not recognize it. When we finally discovered the verse to which he had reference, it was not one I had given him. He had misread my writing and the verse he thought I meant and which had given him such help was one I could scarcely see any value in for personal problems. Yet it had struck him in his own language, and providence had succeeded in spite of me.

Using the Scripture in this manner illustrates the theological basis for the traditional coupling of Scripture with prayer. We think of prayer as conversation with God, but usually in terms of our speaking with him rather than his speaking to us. Through the use of the Scripture as a means of grace God speaks to the believer. In this way the use of Scripture may facilitate the experience of prayer. Prayer has actually begun in this listening activity. After the counselee has listened to God he is moved to speak to God in return. The testimony of the Spirit elicits its response in the believer.

People with problems often gain little satisfaction from their prayers. They carry the same tension into their prayer life that exists in their other activities and call upon God for help in a frame of mind that defies His help. Calvin perceived the self-defeating nature of this kind of prayer when he said of such individuals: "Thus they will come to God, but it is to be at defiance with him, as if a woman should ask something of her husband, and at the same time say, *Oh you care not for me!* . . . Let us learn therefore to pray to God with a peaceable heart."[4] When God is allowed to speak first in prayer, the individual's contribution is likely to show His influence. God works through prayer to change our wills to his.

Scripture homework is the initiation into that communion with God which is the goal of the pastoral counseling process. As such it is the extension of counseling into the devotional life—the counseling relationship with God—that the concept of universal priesthood and the process of sanctification describe. It helps if the pastor points out to the counselee when he assigns the verses to him that listening to God is a form of prayer, that after he has listened to God he should freely express to God whatever comes to his mind at that time. Allowing God to speak first relaxes the counselee so that he has a "peaceable heart" from which to respond to God and with which to receive his grace.

ANALYZING THE METHOD

The specific value to people with problems in this scriptural homework is that they are confronted with the meaning of Jesus Christ for their lives. This calls for a response on their part that is integrating to their personalities. From an analyti-

[4] John Calvin, "How Men Should Pray," in Thomas Kepler (ed.), *The Fellowship of the Saints* (Nashville: Abingdon, 1948), p. 270.

cal viewpoint this integration is facilitated in three ways: mental discipline, positive thinking, and the realization of the presence of God.

a. *Mental discipline.* Because the counselee is often emotionally upset and preoccupied with his problem he has difficulty in controlling his thoughts. He may, for example, read the same page five or six times and still not know what he has read. His state of anxiety so agitates the activity of his mind that he has great difficulty in focusing his attention. Students who have problems can often be spotted before their problem is brought to light by the fluctuation in their schoolwork. Because they are unable to concentrate, their grades go into swift decline. Other occupations show this same slippage in proportion to the amount of mental integration that they require. Naturally the counselee will also experience this difficulty in concentration in his homework with the Scriptures. Consequently the pastor should warn him of what to expect and what to do about it. Every time the counselee becomes consciously aware that his mind has wandered from a verse, he should return it. This procedure must be pursued relentlessly. I usually say something to this effect:

> You will probably find that your mind will wander. Every time it does bring it back to the verse—again and again. The danger is not that your mind will wander, but that you will get discouraged when it does and give up your efforts. Discouragement is your worst enemy. Therefore, learn to recognize it as such. You will only lose your battle when you give up. But if you refuse to give up, you will finally win out.

This value of the homework has little reference to the Bible as the Word of God. I mention it at this point only because it is a helpful by-product of this use of Scripture and because we are in danger of overlooking the value of mental discipline in our contemporary emphasis in psychotherapy. Though such discipline has been confused with the repression of upsetting thoughts and burying rather than solving problems, this does not minimize the value in the conscious rejection of thoughts which are adverse to mental health. In the counseling process there is the permissive atmosphere that encourages self-expression and self-acceptance, and in the counseling homework there is the conscious effort to exercise the "muscles" that have been unknotted in the process of counseling. Both therefore work together as partners and from opposite points of departure to reach the common goal of an integrated mind. This is the fasting (discipline) that Kunkel says must accompany the confession (counseling) for a balanced therapy.

It was my privilege to spend a few months with the class in thought control established by Dr. Joseph B. Pratt at the Boston Dispensary. As a pioneer step in treating patients whose source of illness was emotional rather than organic, this class, now in its third decade, has had a remarkable history in the relief of suffering. The leader of the class, originally Dr. Pratt and at the present time Dr. Paul E. Johnson of Boston University, directs the group to concentrate upon relaxing their bodies, beginning with their toes and working upward to their head. As a climax he directs their thoughts to some scenic view or helpful thought or even a Scripture verse and this concentration is continued for several moments in silence. Through this group therapy of directed thought concentration the tensions that tie up mind and body are eased. Those who need further help receive individual counseling.

In a similar manner the counselee's private reflection on Scripture verses is relaxing to both body and mind. Although the reflection lacks group support to strengthen the integrative effects, it is compensated by the two remaining factors in our analysis.

b. *Positive thinking.* The content of the selected Scriptures is the therapy of the divine message. It contains the answer of God to the problems of men. It is a spiritual tonic to one weakened by internal conflict; a positive infiltration into an otherwise negative way of thinking; a breath of fresh air to an ill-ventilated soul. An old idea is that the way to get rid of the darkness is not to try to sweep it out with a broom but to light a candle. Exposing the mind to the stimulating words of selected Scripture passages is like exposing the skin to the rays of the sun. Not only is it healthy while it is being absorbed but its effects remain to influence the thought processes in the hours ahead. It is the literal practice of St. Paul's formula for mental peace.

> Finally, brethren, whatever is true, whatever is honorable, whatever is just, whatever is pure, whatever is lovely, whatever is gracious, if there is any excellence, if there is anything worthy of praise, think about these things . . . and the God of peace will be with you.

This is the theory behind the therapy of positive thinking. There is danger of both a psychological and theological shallowness in this use of Scripture. Psychologically it may fail to reach the heart of the problem because it is unaccompanied by the confession and insights of the counseling experience. When it is used as homework in conjunction with pastoral counseling, the way is cleared for the Scriptures to achieve the desired effect. Theologically the shallowness consists in viewing Scripture verses as comforting words and thoughts without the inclusion of the dynamic of the encounter with God in the means of grace. The words and thoughts of the Scriptures are therapeutic in a genuine way only when they facilitate the experience of a personal relationship with God. The knowledge revealed through this even makes other issues and events in the life of the counselee understandable. This is the meaning and purpose of revelation and the basis for its integrating power.

c. *Realization of the Presence of God.* Following the interpretation of the doctrine of the means of grace, the use of Scripture as a listening activity is a practical way of bringing God into the counseling process. It presents a tangible way in which the counselee can be instructed to practice the Presence of God. The close association of the message with the Spirit means that one is in a conversational relationship with God when he is listening to the Word. The counselee's realization of this heightens his awareness of the Presence. This can make of the homework activity an experience in that divine-human relationship that is productive of security and confidence. When the message of the verse becomes God speaking to the believer, the separation that generates the destructive emotions is ended in the reunion that produces the fruit of the Spirit.

AREAS OF SPECIAL VALUE

While the use of scriptural homework is helpful whenever the counselee is receptive to the idea there are certain times and conditions where it is especially valuable.

When Counseling is Limited. Although counseling cannot be done in a hurry there are those times in every pastor's ministry when the time factor is a serious limitation. There are always those individuals who put off coming to their pastor until the last minute and even then may bring up their problem only because the circumstances of the interview pressed it to the surface. Tom Henricks for example called to say good-by to his pastor before going back into the service as a reservist. Because his pastor was responsive in his listening, what had appeared to be only a routine farewell turned into a serious counseling situation. The following is an excerpt after one hour of conversation:

TOM: I'm in a terrible mood. I didn't intend to say anything about it, but—maybe it's best this way. Sue broke our engagement. When I told her how much I needed her you'd think she would have a heart—but no. This isn't the first time either. It's always been this way.

PASTOR: This is something you've experienced before.

TOM: Yes. It's humiliating. Get's so a fellow loses his self-respect. Makes you wonder about God too. Does he care? I know that's a terrible question to ask. But—I'm ashamed to say this—but I have to tell somebody. I get to thinking about doing away with myself, and believe me, that's bad.

Naturally this is not a one-interview assignment. Yet Hendricks was leaving the next morning. The pastor devoted himself to the principles of counseling for the greater part of the evening to provide as much release and insight for his counselee as possible. He took his closing moments to explain the procedure for the use of the Bible as a means of grace and to point out its value. Tom indicated his willingness to receive the verses.

On his return six weeks later one of the first things he did was to look up his pastor. He seemed to have gotten a hold on himself.

TOM: I've been getting along pretty good. I'm kind of ashamed of myself for the way I talked before I left. I guess I was pretty down.

PASTOR: I understand how you felt, Tom. And you did what you should—you expressed yourself honestly.

TOM: You know those verses you gave me—they've sure been

a help. I still have a long ways to go—I know that, but I think I know what to do now. I guess something like that is what I've been needing.

Tom undoubtedly still needs counseling to reach the deeper levels of his problem. Yet as he left the parsonage the pastor wondered if he had used the Scriptures as a supplement to his counseling or if his counseling had been the supplement to the Scriptures.

Problems of Faith. Many problems have their repercussions in the spiritual life and are disturbing to one's faith. In the course of counseling with his pastor the counselee may recognize this and desire to strengthen his faith. There is a unity to each problem though it also has its ramifications, and when one phase of the difficulty begins to clear up, its effect will be felt also in the others. If the counselee desires spiritual help and is not using this to prevent his coming to grips with other and perhaps deeper aspects of his problem, the pastor not only has an excellent opening to introduce him to the use of the Word, but has the opportunity presented for a "second front."

When Mrs. Phillips came to her pastor it was to discuss her unhappy marriage. She was an intelligent woman who had taught school several years before her marriage to a man who was unable to share her intellectual interests. Because she was unsatisfied in her desire for companionship she became involved in what was at first an innocent acquaintance with a widowed neighbor, but which ultimately culminated in a series of furtive rendezvous. Her husband found out about it and was deeply shocked. Mrs. Phillips admitted to the pastor that she felt guilty over the whole affair and that she was disturbed over what she felt was a serious decline in her spiritual life.

MRS. PHILLIPS: Frankly my whole spiritual life has slipped. I was brought up right. I suppose this is why I feel so wretched about what has happened.

PASTOR: You have gone against your sense of right and your spiritual life has suffered.

MRS. PHILLIPS: Yes—and then, I've always been one to read a great deal. Perhaps I've read too many books that have caused me to doubt. At any rate God can seem awfully far away. I don't pray as I ought any more. In fact I guess you could say that I don't pray at all. If you could help me with my faith I would appreciate this more than anything else.

Mrs. Phillips had asked for help in her faith. It was an opening to meet her difficulties upon a religious basis. When at the close of the interview the pastor explained to her the relationship of the means of grace both to faith and prayer and the way in which the Scriptures can be used to gain this grace, she seemed quite intrigued with the idea. He also gave her a small book on the intellectual defense of the faith. Because she was deeply conscious of her need, she used the verses faithfully and discovered that a regular devotional program of this nature was not only supportive to her faith, but was of tremendous help in meeting her marital situation.

Making Decisions. The pastor's counselees include those individuals who are faced with an important decision and feel inadequate to make it. If they could just see into the future, they say. If they only knew what was the right thing to do. They fear making the wrong decision; not being sure of their motives, they distrust their own feelings; they seek wisdom. In coming to their pastor they are searching for the will of God in the matter. The pastor, however, is not God, and his adherence to the priesthood of the believer prevents him from mediating the decision. Our inability to know the will of God in this or that matter is often due to the same reason that we receive little benefit from our prayer life. Our frame of mind is a block rather than a help to his guidance. If the counselee devotes some time to concentrating upon the verses of Scripture, regardless of whether they may or may not pertain to the decision, he is exposing his mind to spiritual values. This exposure helps to condition his mind so that it becomes more receptive to God's influence. I explain the procedure to the counselee in approximately this way.

> Our main consideration is to do God's will in this matter. Therefore it's up to us to give him the opportunity to tell us what his will is. This means that we need to expose our minds to his influence so that the way is open for him to speak. In these verses that I am giving you, do not try to twist them to refer to your decision. Simply think upon what the verses have to say in themselves. This gives God the chance to condition the way our mind functions. You are more likely then to think his way in this matter. As you regularly expose yourself in this manner to God, you may notice that one alternative begins to weigh more heavily than the other. If this condition continues, act on it—in faith, of course. As one of the verses says, "We walk not by sight, but by faith."

Nervous People. Since nervousness and worry seem to characterize our age, nervous people are among the pastor's counselees. We usually think of them more as women. The ordeals of child-bearing and raising, more or less insecure marital relations, and menopausal effects all contribute to the problem. Perhaps men merely conceal their fears and frustrations better than women. The high rate of emotionally related organic complications among men may point to this. Burning the candle at both ends, carrying too great a burden too long by oneself, harboring guilt that prevents inner peace, and struggling with the pressures that threaten one's success are the prerogatives of neither male nor female. Even in sleep these individuals receive no rest, for their mind continues its fitful tempo.

The original causes for their inner tension may be so buried by the time they come for counsel that it may no longer be within the scope of the pastor's counseling to unearth them. Yet this does not mean they cannot be helped by his counseling, any more than getting to the root of the problem would guarantee its solution. When the pastor can no longer reach the depths he can still work on the surface. One can learn to handle these personality handicaps and to make the necessary allowances for living with them.

If in addition to the help they receive from counseling they also direct their minds to a structured though unhurried contemplation of the Scriptures, they will experience the change of pace they need. Instead of a continuous process of racing the motor, they are pausing to refuel. It is a temporary breakthrough from this threatening world to the security of the thought of God, and has a stabilizing influence that both reduces the tension and contributes to an easier adjustment to the pressures from within and without.

The Bible can also be used in the actual counseling situation. After the counselee has related an insight, the counselor, instead of giving his usual restatement of that insight, may on occasion correlate the insight with a reference from the Bible. For example, a counselee may say:

COUNSELEE: I get so disgusted with myself, I don't know what to do. I know better than to do what I am doing, but I go ahead and do it anyhow.

PASTOR: You feel like St. Paul did when he said, "The good that I would do I do not, and that which I would not, that I do."

COUNSELEE: Yeah—that's it exactly!

If the counselee appears to show a genuine interest in the correlation, the pastor may give him the reference on a notecard at the close of the session. Or he may locate it in the Bible and allow the counselee to read it for himself. The pastor must restrain himself from overdoing this type of biblical correlation or he will give the impression of preaching. Used occasionally it can stimulate the counselee's interest in the Scriptures and its significance for his problem.

Since there is a limit to the scope of the verbal symbol as an instrument of the Holy Spirit, the sacraments which operate in a different medium were instituted. Of the two—baptism and the Lord's Supper—it is the latter that is of predominant interest to pastoral counseling. Our concluding investigation takes us to this Sacrament of the Altar.

SUMMARY

Although the Bible itself is the sourcebook from the theology of the church rather than an article of this theology, it is the theological doctrine concerning the Bible that presents a plan for its use in pastoral counseling. According to the doctrine of the means of grace the Bible is the means through which God communicates with man. The purpose of the Bible is strictly functional; it is a means to an end and not an end in itself.

The pastor may assign Bible passages which he has selected as homework to the counseling process so that the counselee will hear God speak to him where he needs it most. By explaining the practical application of the doctrine to his problem, the pastor may create within the counselee the desire to engage in this homework. Using the Word in this manner actually exposes an individual's mind to a divine influence which in turn will have its effect on his thought processes in the future. The counselee will see that getting power and wisdom from on high means an obligation on his part of a practical investment of his time and interests with the means of grace.

Because their emotions are usually undisciplined, people with problems may have great difficulty in concentrating. In attempting to focus their thought on a Bible verse they are engaging in an exercise in mental discipline which, in spite of the difficulties involved, will ultimately result in greater discipline and relaxation. Concentrating upon the message of the passage interrupts whatever tendency a person has toward a negative way of thinking. It is a pump primer for the thought patterns that constitute healthy-mindedness. By focusing their attention upon God and what he is saying to them, people with problems are putting themselves in a position to experience the Presence of God. The result is that these periods of listening can become not only highly therapeutic but also most enjoyable.

CHAPTER TWELVE

The Means of Grace

2. THE SACRAMENT IN COUNSELING

> That this is also an ordinary stated means of receiving the grace of God, is evident from the words of the apostle. "The cup of Blessing which we bless, is it not the communion of the blood of Christ? The bread which we break, is it not the communion of the body of Christ?" Is not the eating of that bread, and the drinking of that cup, the outward, visible means, whereby God conveys into our souls all the spiritual grace, that righteousness, and peace, and joy in the Holy Ghost, which were purchased by the body of Christ once broken and the blood of Christ once shed for us? Let all therefore, who truly desire the grace of God, eat of that bread, and drink of that cup.[1]

These words from a sermon of John Wesley seem to sum up with the nearest possible unanimity the theology of the church concerning the Lord's Supper as a means of grace. This sacrament has had a varied history in the life of the church. Beginning with the joyous partaking in conjunction with the love feast in the early church, its celebration took on a more symbolic sacrifice complexion in the late patristic period. In the Middle Ages it became an actual sacrifice supported by the transubstantiation theory. The Reformation broke with this medieval picture to produce a variety of interpretations ranging from commemoration to the real Pres-

[1] John Wesley, *Sermons on Several Occasions* (New York: Phillips and Hunt), I, p. 142.

ence. From that day to this, with the exception of the Anglican communion, the practice of the sacrament has undergone little change in the church families of this era.

The Sacrament is called by many names—Eucharist, Lord's Supper, Last Supper, Sacrament of the Altar, Holy Communion, to name the better known—and each describes one particular purpose of the rite. This variety of function throws a happy light upon the different interpretations of the Sacrament. From the point of view of counseling these various emphases are needed in a balance to make of the sacrament the means of grace the Lord intended it to be. In the controversial setting of this rite instituted as a symbol of unity, each group has so espoused its particular emphasis that it has failed to appreciate the various emphases as a whole. The loss to counseling occurs when any one emphasis is isolated from the others to throw off balance the total impact of the sacrament as a means of grace.

THE HISTORICAL AND THE VISIBLE

When my little girl asked me, "Why can't I see God?" during our family devotions, she was in her childish way expressing a universal human desire. Thomas felt he had to see with his own eyes the risen Christ and put his finger into the nail prints in his hands before he could believe. Or as a counselee told me, "I'd like to find my answer in the love of God, but it's just too intangible." Although we may realize that the spiritual world cannot be experienced in a sensory manner, we are so accustomed to our habitat in a world of material things that the intangible nature of the things of the spirit can be a real problem. In times of stress our faith in the reality of the unseen God and his ways is under assault, and we cry out for something substantial to bolster us. Even though Jesus paid tribute to those who do not see and yet believe, he established the added support that we need. In the Lord's Supper the divine adapts to the human; the spiritual is offered through a tangible medium.

According to the synoptic accounts and that of Paul, Jesus in the night in which he was betrayed took bread and said, "Take, eat: this is my body." In the same manner also he took the cup and said, "Take, drink ye all from it. This cup is the New Covenant in my blood given and shed for you and for many for the remission of sins. This do as oft as ye drink it in remembrance of me." He was instituting a ceremony that would have the sensory appeal of sight and taste and the historical significance of a commemorative drama.

The occasion of the institution adds to its historical moment. It was probably the celebration of the Passover with its roots deep into the ancient religious heritage. The thought that it was the *kiddush*, the evening meal of families before the Sabbath or feast day only enlarges rather than eliminates this Passover orientation. In partaking of the sacrificial lamb, the bitter herbs and the unleavened bread, the Hebrews relived the story of their deliverance from bondage and death in Egypt, when the angel of death passed over their slave hovels with the blood of the lamb on the doorposts. This ceremony of remembrance of divine intervention kept alive their ancient gratitude, and was an inspiration to continue to trust in the guidance of this same Redeemer God. Jesus chose this hour to institute his Supper because it also from a spiritual point of view would be a remembrance of a deliverance from bondage and death, namely the redemption accomplished through his atonement—climaxed also in this Passover season. Thus the old ceremony had its fulfilment in the historical rite of the Lord's Supper and survives in the Christian tradition. It was the Hebrew way of preserving the past in the present through religious observance. Paul bridged this tie between the old and the new when he said, "Christ our Passover Lamb is sacrificed for us." [2]

The memorial emphasis in the sacrament gives to it its anchor in history. By perpetuating in the mind of the participant the original supper and the event it dramatized, the celebration keeps the Jesus of history united with the Christ of the church. By preserving the impressions of the disciples in their contact with Christ, it has prevented the church from going off on a tangent any more than it has from the pioneer and perfector of its faith. Because of its presentation of the gospel in drama the sacrament is called the visible Word. The liturgy that often accompanies the rite, even in Calvinist services, intensifies this medium of communication. As the Word in an act, it bears a unique testimony to the redemptive nature of Christ's work. The symbol has a language all of its own and may reach to a level of personality that words alone would not.

While the commemoration is focused in the crucifixion, it it not confined to it. The work of Christ is a unity in its various events, so that the crucifixion is understood in terms of the incarnation and the resurrection. The worship service in its reliance upon the written Word gives this unity to the commemorative function. In fact it is this particular educative process that prepares the individual for the full perception of the visible Word. The sacrament is the dramatic remembrance that stabilizes the fact that Christianity has a historical rather than a mythological foundation. Even though it is the past that is memorialized, it is a past that extends into the present. The same Christ who broke the bread in the upper room continues to break the bread in the sacrament. The act of the Jesus of history continues as the act of the ascended Lord. As

[2] I Corinthians 5:7.

with the written Word the sacrament becomes effective when the event occurs within the participant in which his spirit is subdued by the Spirit of Christ.

PROTESTANT DIVISIONS

Although the interpretation of the Lord's Supper was the contention that led to the first divisions in Protestantism, the reformers were unified in their awareness of the reassurance in the sacrament. Zwingli understood the sacrament as a memorial feast in which the earthly elements, bread and wine, symbolized the heavenly elements, the body and blood of Christ. To him the ceremony commemorated the sacrifice of Christ as the atonement for sin. In celebrating the Lord's Supper the communicants bring again to their minds the efficacy of this sacrifice. The Zwinglian concept is incorporated in the New Hampshire Confession of the Baptists.

> We believe the Scriptures teach the Lord's Supper is a provision of bread and wine, as symbols of Christ's body and blood, partaken of by the members of the Church, in commemoration of the suffering and death of their Lord; showing their faith and participation in the merits of His sacrifice, and their hope of eternal life through His resurrection from the dead; its observance to be preceded by faithful self-examination.

Calvin went further than Zwingli. He too felt the bread and wine symbolized the body and blood of Christ, but he also saw in the sacrament another symbol. The *partaking* of the bread and wine symbolized the spiritual receiving of the heavenly elements. Bread and wine were the staff of life in food and drink in Jesus' day. As the bread and wine nourish the body, so the spiritual reception of the body and blood of Christ nourishes the soul. For Calvin this analogy is not only a symbol, but a description of reception. He referred to the sacraments as a pedagogy of signs to strengthen faith—a certification of the promise of the gospel. He also referred to them as means of grace. The bread and wine are the conveyors of the spiritual presence of Christ. The Thirty-nine Articles of the Episcopal Church convey this Calvinist interpretation.

The Supper of the Lord is not only a sign of the love that Christians ought to have among themselves one to another; but rather it is a Sacrament of our Redemption by Christ's death: insomuch that to such as rightly, worthily, and with faith, receive the same, the Bread which we break is a partaking of the Body of Christ; and likewise the Cup of blessing is a partaking of the Blood of Christ . . . The Body of Christ is given, taken and eaten, in the Supper, only after an heavenly spiritual manner. And the means whereby the Body of Christ is received and eaten in the Supper, is Faith.

Luther saw more than symbol in the bread and wine. He believed they were the earthly carriers of the body and blood of Christ. He saw also more than symbolical partaking of the heavenly element; as the bread and wine are orally received into the body, they carry with them in a "heavenly manner" the body and blood of Christ to the soul. The sacrament has objective reality in both its seen and unseen elements. Even the unbeliever receives the body and blood in the Sacrament, not however to his benefit, but to his judgment. The partaker's faith does not condition the sacrament, but rather conditions a beneficial reception of the sacrament. To Luther the benefit of the sacrament was in the words, "given and shed for you for the remission of sins." It is a means of grace in that the heavenly elements are received for the strengthening of faith. Through its visible sign there is the assurance of personal forgiveness. Luther's Small Catechism embodies Luther's teaching on the sacrament.

The Sacrament of the Altar is the true body and blood of our Lord Jesus Christ, under the bread and wine, given unto us Christians to eat and to drink, as it was instituted by Christ Himself. The benefit of such eating and drinking is pointed out in these words: "Given and shed for you for the remission of sins." Through these words the remission of sins, life and salvation are given unto us in the Sacrament; for where there is remission of sins, there is also life and salvation.

The practice of the Lord's Supper in the Zwinglian tradition offers more opportunity for the partaker to offer himself in the same spirit of self-giving in which he was received. The Calvinistic rite emphasizes the real Presence of Christ as the Eternal High Priest of the distribution in which he gives himself. Luther linked the Presence to the earthly elements, something Calvin could not do. The difference between the Calvin and Zwinglian views and that of Luther rests upon the Lutheran doctrine of ubiquity. To Calvin and Zwingli Christ was too transcendent in his body to be received through the elements. For Luther Christ in his body is everywhere present. Thus the Calvin-Zwingli view makes difficult any sacramental presence as such, because of the gulf fixed between the tangible and intangible worlds. Essentially Luther's view is simply a denial of this gulf between the two worlds. Consequently we find in Luther a greater element of mystery.

COMMUNION

The sense of mystery is involved because of the real Presence, for whenever God is revealed to the human soul there also is mystery, for the human is limited in its perception of the divine. For this reason St. Paul warns of the danger of profaning the sacrament and urges steps to prevent it.

Whoever, therefore, eats the bread or drinks the cup of the Lord in an unworthy manner will be guilty of profaning the body and blood of the Lord. Let a man examine himself, and so eat of the bread and drink of the cup. For any one who eats and drinks without discerning the body eats and drinks judgment upon himself.[3]

The sacrament can be compared to the incarnation. As the

[3] I Corinthians 11:27-29.

two natures of Christ, the human and the divine, are united in his person, so in the sacrament the human elements are united with the divine. As Luther pointed out, no transubstantiation was necessary to receive the divine through the human in the incarnation, so none is required for the reception of the divine through the human in the sacrament. There is no necessity for thinking of the body and blood in terms of sensory perception, for the whole process is a mediation of a union with Christ in the deep places of the soul. The mystery or revelation of his presence is in the sacrament as a whole—as the One who says, "Take, eat"; it is conveyed through the elements—"The cup of blessing which we bless, is it not a participation in the blood of Christ?"; it is manifested in the church which is his visible body in the world.

It is in partaking that the sacrament becomes communion. This is the second part of the rite, the first being the memorial drama. Jesus through his death would enter the realm of the spirit where he could live within the believer. The sacrament is a means Jesus chose to communicate himself. As such it is a vivid way of practicing the Presence. Even the two-way nature of communion is involved, for viewing the sacrament from its human pole, it is also an enactment of the believer's approach to God through Jesus Christ. Through it the Spirit bears witness with our spirit that we are the children of God and makes intercession for us with groanings that cannot be uttered. As a means of grace the sacrament communicates Christ but is not Christ. God is the master of his means.

EUCHARIST

The expression of thanksgiving was so prominent in the celebration of the Lord's Supper in the early days of the church that the Greek word for thanksgiving, eucharist, became synonymous with the rite. Through the atonement of

Christ God had triumphed over the forces of evil; through the forgiveness of sins the believer realized the fellowship of God. Here was cause for great rejoicing. This eucharistic emphasis in the sacrament places the element of thanksgiving in its rightful role at the center of worship. The church of the apostles had a radiance that later ages were not able to retain. "And day by day, attending the temple together and breaking bread in their homes, they partook of food with glad and generous hearts, praising God and having favor with all the people." [4] To them the gospel was so new that it was still good news and their spontaneity of joy dominated their celebration of the sacrament.

There is danger that in an overemphasis on mystery and the necessity for penitence, the communicant may miss this experience of praise and thanksgiving in the rite. When the emphasis on commemoration turns the celebration into a duty there is this same danger. The prominence that is given to thanksgiving in the sacrament emphasizes the importance of gratitude in the spiritual life and of the gospel as the basis for this gratitude. The foundation for Christian gratitude does not depend upon this or that particular blessing which may come and go. It is gratitude for God himself, and specifically, for Christ. This helps us to understand how St. Paul could make thanksgiving a constant possibility.

> Have no anxiety about anything, but in everything by prayer and supplication with thanksgiving let your requests be made known to God. And the peace of God, which passes all understanding, will keep your hearts and minds in Christ Jesus.[5]

It shows also the role of the sacrament in the relief of anxiety through its impressive assurance of good news.

[4] Acts 2:46-47.
[5] Philippians 4:6-7.

THE BOND OF FELLOWSHIP

The Lord's Supper is a symbol of another communion—the communion of saints. The unity of Christians is demonstrated by the common table and is made an actual experience by the sharing together of the body of Christ; those who become united with their Lord in the sacrament also become united with each other. As St. Paul said, "Because there is one loaf, we who are many are one body, for we all partake of the same loaf." Luther enlarges upon this figure:

> To symbolize this fellowship, God has appointed such signs of the sacrament as in every way serve this purpose and by their very form incite and move us to this fellowship. Just as the bread is made out of many grains which have been ground and mixed together, and out of the many bodies of grain there comes the one body of the bread, in which each grain loses its form and body and acquires the common body of the bread, and as the drops of wine losing their own form become the body of one wine: so should it be with us, and is, indeed, if we use this sacrament aright.[6]

The early church which was known for its bond of fellowship celebrated the sacrament together with the *agape* or love feast, even as Jesus ate his fellowship meal with his disciples. It was the corruption of this love feast by overindulgence and strife in the church at Corinth that precipitated Paul's exposition of the sacrament in that letter. The *agape* continued until nearly 400 A.D. on Maundy Thursday, the anniversary of the historic meal. The Church of the Brethren and a few smaller groups continue to follow this custom in celebrating the sacrament.

During the Middle Ages this fellowship emphasis was lost in the concentration upon the infusion of grace to the individual communicant.[7] This same overemphasis upon the

[6] Martin Luther, "Treatise on the Blessed Sacrament," *op. cit.*, II, p. 17.

[7] For a detailed study of the history of the sacrament see Yngve Brilioth's scholarly *Eucharistic Practice, Evangelical and Catholic* (London: Society for the Promotion of Christian Knowledge, 1930).

individual to the detriment of fellowship is always a danger among those churches that stress the mystery of the sacrament. The tension between the individual and the corporate is preserved only as the individual is conscious that he partakes as a part of a fellowship and the fellowship is concerned that the individual is blessed in the experience. The original meaning of the church as the *ekklesia* is synonymous with this fellowship; in the Apostles' Creed the communion of saints is in apposition to the Holy Christian (Catholic) Church. When churches lose this fellowship, and people come and go without becoming conscious of any communion of saints, the group solidarity is gone and the bond of union symbolized in the sacrament is an empty form. What has happened to the churches has had its effect on church members since personality problems develop in an atmosphere of isolation.

The sacrament brings the members of the fellowship to the essential meaning of Christianity. Whatever differences may have existed beforehand between the individuals are lost in the presence of the self-giving sacrifice of God. It is here that Calvin sees the strongest incentive to live the Christian life. As the fellowship partakes of the sacrifice of love that binds it together, the members themselves are drawn to each other by the rise of that same sacrificial love within themselves. Such a strengthening of the bond of union should have its effect also in the smaller units of this fellowship such as family relationships. There are churches where it is not uncommon to see members rise from their pew before the celebration of the sacrament to shake the hand of a brother with whom there has been dissension. The church as a whole has usually requested those who refuse to be reconciled with their brethren to abstain from the sacrament, since their very attitude is a division in the body that the sacrament would belie.

When the communicant visualizes the scene in the upper room, Jesus with the twelve, and in spirit joins them in partaking of the elements, he is part of that body of kindred souls who have re-enacted this event for nearly two thousand years. Here is a fellowship that is undisturbed by the limitations of space or time—or even denominations. In all of this there is a sense of belonging that is unsurpassed and a reassurance that is inspiring. This is the sentiment and the purpose behind World Communion Sunday.

COVENANT WITH ETERNITY

The two sacraments are joined by the covenant between God and man based upon the redeeming work of Christ. In baptism the covenant is ratified and in the Lord's Supper it is reaffirmed. God on his part promises the believer "the forgiveness of sins, life and salvation," and the believer affirms his trust in this promise and in gratitude dedicates his life to God. The scope of the covenant extends into eternity; the end of God's promise is everlasting life. Jesus associated this eschatological phase of the covenant with the sacrament when he said following the distribution that he would not drink again from the cup until he drank it anew with them in his Father's kingdom. In the sacrament the historical and the eternal are united, and the communicant is renewed in his faith in the life beyond and in its fulfilment of all the good in the life that is temporal.

This emphasis on the eternal hope is associated by St. Paul with a confession of faith. "As often as you eat this bread and drink the cup, you proclaim the Lord's death until he comes." [8] It is a profession before all who witness of the participant's hope in the sacrifice of Christ. Accompanying this reaffirmation of the covenant is the reception of the gift

[8] I Corinthians 11:26.

that stabilizes the covenant. In the sacramental nature of the drama the elements of the sacrifice that was broken and shed for the remission of sins are received into the soul as reassurance to the believer of his oneness with his Creator. This is the spiritual sustenance that quickens the participant. Actually therefore the Lord's Supper is a buttress to the doctrine of justification by grace through faith; a tangible reassurance of the covenant that puts an end to guilt and its consequences for time and eternity.

THE CONFESSION OF SINS

The celebration of Communion has historically been preceded by a spiritual preparation on the part of the communicants. For most churches this takes the form of simple confession of sins or a confessional service. Already in the early church the confession of sin preceded the actual service of the Eucharist. The probable origin of this practice is the exhortation of St. Paul to the Corinthians to examine themselves before eating of the bread and drinking of the cup to avoid any profaning of the sacrament. Confession also is a logical preparation for the assurance of forgiveness. Joined by the support of the fellowship, the therapy of the confessional service is increased. Although practices differ, it usually has three ingredients: confession, forgiveness, and intention.

Confession. If the participant is at all serious in his intent to examine himself, he may to some extent face his personal deficiencies. To encourage this, most services include words from the Scripture that point to these deficiencies. The preparatory service of the Evangelical and Reformed Church uses the Ten Commandments for this purpose. The probability is that the confessor is also accepting at least some of the responsibility for his sins. The fact that his counselor in this instance is God increases his chances for being honest with himself, since the very idea of God implies that nothing can be hidden from him. In this moment of honest introspection he may gain insight into his personality.

But there is danger of distortion. A parishioner came to his pastor disturbed over the fact that he did not feel penitent as he should during the confession before Communion. The pastor pointed out to him that he really was penitent over not feeling penitent and this brought him to a temporary satisfaction. Because of their unresolved destructive emotions, people may twist these characteristics of a receptive spirit into attitudes which they must conjure up as credentials for receiving that which is given by grace.

Forgiveness. After the communicant has been asked to face his failures he is offered a way of redemption. When he acknowledges his sins he hears the good news that God forgives. The offer of forgiveness to which he listens is from the doctrine of the atonement about to be sacramentally demonstrated in the Communion. Hearing that God accepts him as he is encourages him to accept himself.

Intention. The sincerity of the communicant is put to the test: "Do you resolve to submit yourself in the future to the gracious direction of the Holy Spirit so that you may no more purposely sin, but be enabled to follow after holiness?" This question impresses upon him his responsibilities. It is the expression of his self-oblation in response to the covenant of God. Since lack of self-discipline may be one of his shortcomings, this question could also frustrate him, were it not asked in view of the help of the Holy Spirit. Here is a promise of a partnership that inspires faith in progress and hope for the future. In becoming aware of his dependence upon God he is indirectly gaining confidence in himself.

In many churches the congregation participates aloud in the confessional service which makes it more personal and adds to it the therapy of self-expression. Also included in the service of preparation is some form or other of the pastoral use of the office of the keys. In his official position as a called and ordained minister of Christ, the pastor pronounces the absolution to the penitent. This is based on Jesus' post-resurrection commission to His disciples: "If you forgive the sins of any, they are forgiven; if you retain the sins of any, they are retained."[9] Here it is from the Evangelical and Reformed service:

Hearken now unto the comforting assurance of the grace of God, promised in the Gospel to all that repent and believe: As I live, saith the Lord God, I have no pleasure in the death of the wicked, but that the wicked turn from his way and live. God so loved the world that he gave his only begotten Son, that whosoever believeth in him should not perish, but have everlasting life. Wherefore, beloved brethren, those of you who have truly turned to God with hearty repentance and sincere faith, may assuredly believe that your sins are forgiven; through Jesus Christ our Lord. Amen.

THE SACRAMENT AND PROBLEMS

The use of reassurance in pastoral counseling is under criticism because it has been overdone. Pastors have given reassurance prematurely, even before they have unearthed the problem, and have given it ineffectually, using only the verbal approach. In the desire to encourage counselees, pastors have too often smoothed on salve when the sore needed to be lanced. Yet there is both a need and a place for reassurance. Because of the frailties of man and the frustrations of everyday living the problem of guilt is a recurring thing. It maintains a terrific hold on the human personality so that even in forgiveness it has its remnants that may continue to exert a destruc-

[9] John 20:23.

tive influence. The way of forgiveness described in the confessional service is the church's answer to this disturbing power. The solution to a problem so fundamental to the ills of the soul and so deep in its penetration of personality needs continual fortification. In the sacrament of the Lord's Supper there is added to the assurance of the Word an actual participation in the drama of redemption. Following the invitation to take and eat, the communicant in the re-enactment claims this forgiveness as his own by taking it into his very soul. This is done repeatedly in the Christian life because of the ever-pressing necessity to continue the attack on guilt—until all the Canaanites have been driven from the promised land. For whatever remains shall become thorns in the side.

In addition to the reassurance of forgiveness for the offensive against guilt there are the other functions of the sacrament that contribute to the ministry of pastoral counseling. The commemoration of the historical anchor of the Christian hope has a strengthening effect upon this hope in the believer. The things that are seen in the sacrament are a tangible support for the communicant's faith in the things that are not seen, for which they serve as vehicles. The dramatic reception in the rite heightens the reality of the divine Presence and encourages the participant's experience of communion with Christ. The eucharistic emphasis is both a stimulus to and an expression of the central Christian note of praise and thanksgiving—so beneficial to the health of personality. The unity of the body of Christ which is demonstrated in the common partaking of the bread gives to the communicant the sense of solidarity that decreases the activity of the destructive emotions. The reaffirmation of the covenant that structures the individual's relationship with God stabilizes the participant in the security of this relationship and inspires him to love as he has been loved. These functions of the sacrament in their total effect not only express the triumph of the redemption in Christ, but are the necessary invigorants for the soul in conflict.

In its purpose as a reassurance and an invigorant, the Lord's Supper not only is a stabilizing influence in emotional disturbances but may also avert these disturbances. Its role is more of a preventative of problems and a support in recuperation than a cure. When a counselee has confessed to a sin over which he feels extremely guilty and the application of the doctrine of justification has not been completely successful in conveying the assurance of acceptance, the Christian may find in the sacrament the extra force that is needed. Jim Cotton was in his late teens when he broke down and confessed his guilt over masturbation. His initial problem was a terrible fear that he could not account for. Through the pastor's responsive listening he was able to uncover his shame. Among religious young people this particular guilt can be most severe. Jim felt corrupted and even when he left the pastor's study his guilt was unalleviated. When he returned the following week he felt much differently.

JIM: When I left here last week I felt terrible, even though you tried to assure me of forgiveness. It was awful for the next couple of days. I wished over and over again I had never told you. Then Sunday, as you know, we had Communion. After I took it, it seemed like something lifted off my back. As though God were forgiving me–really.

Addiction to masturbation is a symptom of an emotional disturbance rather than the problem itself, and often serves as an escape mechanism. The pastoral counseling experience has much yet to accomplish for Jim before he is on his way to complete recovery. Yet his feeling of acceptance is the step in this direction that is basic to the whole recovery process. Without the preceding counseling, however, he might not have received this support in Communion.

In fact people who are having serious problems may avoid Communion. This is particularly true in those churches that emphasize the solemnity of the rite. Pastors have been indebted to this sacrament many times for bringing to their attention the problems of the congregation. A pastor newly installed in his congregation and not as yet familiar with his people, noticed in the distribution of the elements during a communion service, a woman whose countenance showed the strain of emotional conflict. When she was offered the cup her hand began to shake and she could not bring herself to take and drink. The pastor followed up the clue and soon was ministering in an acute family discord.

Gerald Johnson was a life-of-the-party type of an individual whose gay appearance and levity were a source of good humor to his friends, but he became disturbed over himself and sought out his pastor for counsel.

JOHNSON: I seem to be living all on the surface. I sometimes wonder if I have any inner life. I'm realizing more and more that my clowning is just a way of getting a lot of laughs that keep *me* going.

During the second interview Gerald expressed another insight.

JOHNSON: My life seems to be two extremes. Funny I hadn't seen this before. Usually I'm clowning and can't take anything serious, but there have been times when I'm just the opposite.

Although Johnson talked freely, the pastor and he did not seem to get anywhere in locating the cause of his two natures.

PASTOR: Can you describe when such a time might be when you are in your other extreme?

JOHNSON: (pause) Yes, I believe I can. It's often at Communion. I feel heavy and weighted down—as though I didn't belong there. I couldn't joke then if I had to. It's like I was immersed in seriousness.

PASTOR: As though you felt unworthy.

JOHNSON: Yeah—unworthy—that describes it right on the nose. There are other times at Communion, though, when I can't take it seriously at all.

This was the lead they needed to give direction to the search. Johnson's levity was an escape from a deeply buried feeling of guilt over himself, which would rise to the surface on rare occasions, but would shortly be submerged by the return of the levity to prevent any conscious recognition of the problem he had not wanted to face.

Keeping a communion record is also a help, since it brings to the pastor's attention those who are staying away from the sacrament. A reminder to Mr. G., a man about sixty years of age and a nominal church member, that he had not communed in over a year brought an unusual response. He became extremely angry and was so emotionally upset that he could not sleep. When the pastor heard of his reaction he called at his home. Mr. G. in an emotional tirade released his resentment against the church, against God, and against life itself. The thought of the intimacy of God's presence in the sacrament was repelling to his resentful feelings toward God. Like most church people, however, he recoiled at the thought of resenting God. He kept his conflict in check by not letting his left hand know what his right hand was doing—by preventing his ambivalent feelings from meeting together in his consciousness. Staying away from Communion was part of this subconscious mechanism of protection. His infuriation at the pastor's reminder showed that it had broken through the barricade and exposed his escape from himself.

When people are having problems and difficulties they often feel ashamed over them. Because they feel hypocritical in dining at the Lord's Table, they avoid it. There is a danger that the pastor will not recognize in this avoidance a symptom of a deep problem and will think that his primary task is to urge the delinquent to more frequent partaking. He may do more harm than good. If these people partake in the Communion they may feel they have communed unworthily and their guilt will be increased rather than decreased. As a result they are further removed from the help of the church than before. There is the danger with the sacrament as with Scripture and prayer that the pastor may subconsciously think of it as an escape from the responsibility of counseling rather than as a resource in counseling.

In the counseling relationship the problem can be dislodged from its inner entanglements and can be looked at objectively. When a person has an understanding of his problem and insight into how he can solve it, he is on his way to recovery. His recuperation can be slow, however, as it hits snags along the way that cause discouragement and even failure. If he were reinforced at these danger points it would help to insure his recuperation and certainly speed its progress. The sacrament can be this reinforcement. It is the divine refreshment that is needed in this shaky period of faltering recovery. As a means of grace based on the Word, the doctrine of the Lord's Supper prescribes the use of the sacrament as a resource in pastoral counseling.

THE USE OF THE SACRAMENT IN COUNSELING

How then can the pastor use the sacrament as the needed fortification in the recuperation of his counselee? Both the Word and the sacrament are means of grace. As with the

Word, however, the way the sacrament is administered affects its influence. Although two preachers speak from the same text, one may move his congregation and the other may not. The deciding factor is the way they present their message. So also the manner in which the pastor approaches the sacrament influences the attitudes of his people. Does he conduct the ceremony with his counselees in mind or with the lifelessness of a perfunctory ritual? If he understands the therapy in the sacrament and concentrates upon this during the service he will administer it in a way that encourages this therapy.

A communion service should be impressive; it should inspire reverence. The effective use of music can do much toward creating this atmosphere. People must be mentally prepared for an experience of reverence. We speak of the liturgical and nonliturgical churches in Protestantism, but in Communion there is a common liturgy. The words of institution and the distribution of the elements are the prescribed form from the upper room. Even in the informal churches of the Baptist family there is a repetition of this ritual together with the prayer of remembrance and the prayer of thanksgiving. So the liturgy of the upper room perpetuates the continuity with the past, which is in a sense what all liturgy does.

The liturgy of the church and the theology of the church are closely related. In matters such as the Lord's Supper the liturgy may express more fully than the theology the religious experience that is described. Like the sacrament it is structured within the framework of the worship experience, with its appeal to emotion as well as reason. For this reason liturgy has escaped the contortions of controversy and consequently retains in these controversial areas the more positive expression of personal religious experience. From the earliest days the church has built up a rich liturgical heritage around the Lord's Supper. It is of interest that the churches who espouse the Zwinglian concept of the Supper are some of the most nonliturgical churches while Zwingli himself was quite liturgically minded compared with Calvin. Whether with the historic forms of the church's past—the Sursum Corda, Preface, Sanctus, Agnus Dei—or with the form recorded in the Synoptic Gospels, the pastor must vitalize the forms with the atmosphere of worship and devotion so that the congregation is receptive to the Presence of Christ.

The psychological build-up for the sacrament begins in the sermon. If the Communion is the climax of the service of the day, the entire service should be integrated around it. This may of course not be necessary among those churches which celebrate the Communion every Sunday. In the sermon the pastor has an excellent opportunity not only to create an anticipation for the sacrament but also to explain the purpose and benefit of the sacrament. Even as the use of the Word is facilitated by an explanation of its function, so the experience of Communion is enhanced by a description of its meaning and purpose.

Protestant churches have suffered from the naive reaction that a knowledge of theology is at best only incidental to the quality of religious experience, as though religion were the one exception to the value of education for the enrichment of experience. What is needed is a revitalized education in the heritage of the church—its doctrines and its worship. If a former generation suffered from an overdose of legalistic dogmatism our present doctrinal vacuity does not remedy the situation. The intellect is a door, not the only door but an important door, for the stimulation of experience, and when the door is enlarged by a liturgical setting such as the Lord's Supper it is a tremendous opening into the heart of man. The more a person consciously understands the meaning of those things that are spiritually perceived, the more meaning they will have for him. As people are psychologically prepared for the therapy of the sacrament they are in a frame of mind receptive to this therapy. The sacrament that was meant for sinners will give its unique consolation to those who sigh under the weight of their guilt; those who stumble in spirit will find their strength in its heavenly sustenance.

Churches differ in their frequency of the celebration of the Communion from once a week to three or four times a year. In churches with infrequent communions the pastor may use the sacrament quite effectively in a private manner in his counseling. The background for the private use of communion is the sick-room communion practiced by certain churches. Its use can be expanded to include also the sick in soul. Practices differ, since some churches feel individual communion is in order while others believe at least two should commune. Although the group support in the church communion would be ostensibly absent, the private communion is conducted under conditions similar to the counseling relationship and therefore suggestive of the problem and its solution. The fact that the Communion joins one not only to the fellowship within his local church but with the entire church means that when a person communes privately he is still communing as a member of the church and the fellowship is no less a reality than when it is visibly represented in a congregation.

When a congregation has been educated to the purpose in the sacrament a counselee may even ask for Communion. Mrs. Evans had been keeping her marital problems within the confines of her own home for a long time and finally could bear them no longer and came for help. She broke down and in shame told of her suspicions of her husband's infidelity. For years the two had been drifting apart and now it seemed there was scarcely any marriage left. She admitted that she had not been a responsive wife and had not always been easy to live with. At the same time she felt rather helpless to do anything. She decided that she would try again to have a heart-to-heart talk with her husband in an effort to save their marriage.

About a week later she called her pastor and asked if he could come to their house and give them Communion. He went without question. Although nothing was said about their trouble it was obvious that the celebration of Communion was the seal of a new covenant that each was making with the other and with God. It was a sacred moment of forgiveness and reconciliation in the intimacy of their home, and undoubtedly had its effect on the endurance of the new life.

SUMMARY

From the study of psychotherapy we know that guilt feelings which have any age or depth are extremely difficult to overcome, and even when they are discharged they may return upon minor provocation. Also we are continually operating our lives in ways that create new guilt feelings. Christ instituted the sacrament of his Supper as a reinforcement of the doctrine of justification for the removal of guilt. Even as the doctrine of justification is based upon the atonement, so the Sacrament of the Altar is in effect a dramatization of the atonement.

The Lord's Supper offers the tangible as a buttress for the intangible. Bread and wine can be seen and tasted; their distribution is connected with a historical event; the scene in the upper room can be visualized and relived. The reception of the heavenly elements of the atonement in a heavenly manner in the sacrament signifies that the forgiveness of sins is received into the very substance of the soul. To make the reassurance of the sacrament more effective the ceremony is preceded by a re-evaluation of the participant's need for forgiveness, so that no vestige of guilt may remain uninfluenced by the reassurance, that his peace of soul may become an increasingly permanent possession.

The doctrine of the Lord's Supper readily ties the pastoral counseling program into the worship program of the church. In so doing it prevents pastoral counseling from becoming an isolated area of the ministry. It can substitute for no other activity of the ministry and its success is dependent upon the entire program of the ministry. The beliefs of the layman show a correlation to what he hears from the pulpit. The theology that unites pastoral counseling with the total ministry is united with it also in its purpose. Working together they can be an effective combination for the relief of human problems.

CONCLUSION

We have been alerted to the need for training pastors in the sound principles of clinical psychology. A need just as urgent is for pastors who are trained in using the resources of the theology of the church in their personal counseling. I have witnessed the tremendous value of this practical application of the doctrines of the church for helping people. But mine is a trivial testimony. Countless multitudes in the centuries of time have experienced the power in this heritage of Christendom for healing and health. The theory and theology of pastoral counseling are tools in pastoral counseling, even as the theory and the theology of homiletics are tools in preaching. In both we need to rely upon the God behind the tools. For he is greater than either theory or theology. We are dependent upon him for the wisdom, guidance and power in our use of the tools and for our success with them.

Type used in this book

Body, 11 on 14 and 11 on 12 and 9 on 11 Janson

Display, Radiant